Shattered

Picking Up the Pieces

Rosemary Harris

Copyright © 2025 by Rosemary Harris

All rights reserved. No part of this publication may be reproduced, distributed, or transmitted in any form or by any means, including photocopying, recording, or other electronic or mechanical methods, without the prior written permission of the publisher, except as permitted by U.S. copyright law.

I've represented events as faithfully as possible. This memoir contains memories and events from my personal perspective. For privacy reasons, some names, locations, and dates may have been changed.

Cover design by Kingofdesigner, commissioned via Fiverr

Photographer: JCPenney Portraits (Robbie D.)

Library of Congress Control Number: 2025912999

ISBN: 979-8-218-61249-8

Printed in the United State of America

Dedication

To all those who are healing and on their journey of self-discovery:
May you find strength in your struggles, wisdom in your experiences, and peace in your heart.
This is for you—a reminder that every step you take brings you closer to the person you are meant to be.

Preface

This book came about at a very dark time in my life. My relationship of 10 years was over. The man that I was in love with stopped speaking to me, and I was in therapy because I was trying to heal from childhood and adulthood traumas. These included: molestation, date rape, and an abusive relationship that lasted for almost seven years. I was also trying to heal from my failed relationships.

In December 2021, I was lying in bed sad and disappointed that the man I loved had stopped communicating with me. Although I had my son, I felt alone. I always wanted to write a book, but I did not know this was how it would play out. I pulled out my phone and started typing away on my iPhone 13 Plus in the "Notes" app. As I was writing, I was angry, disappointed, and crying. I stayed up until 4 a.m. writing, and when I finally stopped typing, I felt like someone had lifted a heavy weight from me. At that moment, I knew that after 41 years, it was time to sit in my truth and tell my story.

I hope my story helps other women who have been through similar experiences feel brave enough to speak out and sit in their truth. I want my story to be an educational tool for teenage girls, so they are more equipped to prevent some of these things from happening in the first place.

As I was writing this book, I learned a lot about myself. I now know I'm strong, and my experiences and mistakes do not define who I am as a human being, a woman, or a mother. Slowly, with therapy, I'm healing. I can look at myself in the mirror and know that I am worthy of love, that I am enough, and that I should always be treated with respect by anyone who wants to be in my life.

I no longer feel ashamed or guilty. Writing this book has given me back so much confidence.

Contents

Introduction	1
1. The Beginning	3
2. Shattered	15
3. Too Good to Be True	39
4. Picking Up the Pieces	69
5. Conclusion	93
6. Acknowledgements	94
7. A Letter to the Reader	97
About the author	99

Introduction

As far back as I can remember, I was always a daddy's girl. There wasn't anything like spending those hot summer afternoons with my dad, in the kitchen making lunch for my sister and me. He would take us to Highland Park to play, or up the street to our neighborhood park before he went to work at a nearby hospital. My mom would have already gone early in the morning to work in the nursing industry on the other side of town.

Throughout the years, we had a couple of babysitters while our parents worked, and we were latch-key kids. One summer, our aunt Diana, my dad's brother's wife, watched my sister and me. That was when I had my innocence stripped from me.

My uncle had two biological kids then, and a stepdaughter named Melissa, who was older than her siblings as well as my sister and me. I was around six years old, and she was around eleven. One day, we were playing hide-and-seek. Melissa told me to hide with her in the bedroom closet. When we got into that closet she proceeded to touch me in places no one should touch a 6-year-old. I felt weird and knew it was wrong. This had happened on more than one occasion; it took place the whole summer. She told me not to tell anyone, or she would beat me up. Being six years old, I was scared because she was older and bigger than me.

I never told anyone what happened until my friend Quincy asked me on June 28, 2019, "What are your demons, Rose?" I told Quincy that I was molested by a female cousin when I was younger, but there were many more demons I had. At 41, it was time to own my truth, heal from it, and tell my story.

I hope that telling my story will help many others who've experienced sexual abuse, domestic violence, and date rape to come forward and/or to get the help they need to be able to heal and live a happier, more fulfilling life.

Now, please fasten your seat belt because I'm about to take you on the rollercoaster ride you would never want to be on.

The Beginning

I come from a middle-class, two-parent household. My parents met at Westview Amusement Park in 1976 and married on January 3, 1978, at the Allegheny County Courthouse, with my grandfather as their only witness. My mom's mother wasn't happy about my mom marrying my dad, so she did not show up.

My mom became pregnant with me at 24 years old. I was born on Sunday, June 22, 1980, at Magee Women's Hospital in Pittsburgh, Pennsylvania. I was a beautiful baby with caramel skin, slanted brown eyes, chubby cheeks, and a full head of black silky hair. My dad is the one who named me. I'm named after my dad's mom, Rose, and my mom, Mary—two strong women who both experienced their share of pain and disappointments.

A year later, on September 10, 1981, they welcomed my sister Natalie. My parents had their two girls, and we were one big happy family. As little kids, we spent a lot of days at my maternal grandparents' house in the Homewood area of Pittsburgh. This was in the 1980s, and it was a beautiful, thriving Black community with big homes and big cars parked out front. My grandparents were both from the South; my grandfather was from North Carolina, and my grandmother was from Georgia. They had a garden with a few other neighbors. They would work in 'the field' for hours, and we kids would help, but mostly play.

I had a lot of cousins. There were eight of us: four boys and four girls. Two of my male cousins, Sam and Sylvester, were brothers, and I had another male cousin, Leonard, who was born four months after me. His little brother Lionel was only a baby at this time. As we got older, our male cousins would try to grab what wasn't breast yet, or touch our butts. Every time I went to my grandparents' house, this would happen. I never said anything, nor did my sister or other female cousins.

Even some of their male friends who would come to play would touch us in inappropriate ways, too! No one ever told an adult. We were too afraid to say something. They silenced us with the fear of beating us up. This behavior went on for years, and one day, it stopped when I reached the sixth grade. My cousins were now older and had a girlfriend or girlfriend(s). At the time, I was old enough to decide to stay home alone when my mom would go there to visit.

I would go years without seeing my family members. At the time of this writing in December 2021, the last time I encountered anyone from that side of the family was when my grandmother passed away in March 2018. I'm not even friends with any of my cousins on social media except for one, but he was younger and would never visit our grandparent's house.

Middle School

I remember starting middle school in 1991. It was nice that my middle school had a summer camp for a month so we could get to know some of our peers before the beginning of the school year started. When September rolled around for the first day of school, I wasn't scared since I made friends at the summer camp.

The first time someone inappropriately touched me at school, it was these two boys, Derrick and Charles. Derrick lived in my neighborhood, and we went to elementary school together. They both sat at my table for language arts class. They both would make inappropriate statements about my breast or butt, and it always made me feel weird and awkward. I would politely ask them to stop, but they would continue to laugh and comment, so I was happy when the teacher agreed that it would be best to move my seat. That put an end to their disrespectful behavior.

I wasn't one of the popular girls, so I was excited when a boy named Jimmy, who was in all my classes, asked if I wanted to be friends. Then there was Paul, a boy I met at summer camp, and we became friends, too! Paul and Jimmy were best friends and had known each other since elementary school. One morning while at my locker, each one ran passed and smacked me on my butt. Since about the age of 10, I have had a bigger backside than most girls my age. One time, even a grown man remarked how big my backside was. My mom cussed that man out and was about to beat him down, and go to jail for it. I was angry that Jimmy and Paul did that, and I thought it was a one-time thing. But they would do this until we graduated from middle school. Our associate principal caught them doing it one time and pulled us all into her office, explaining to them the seriousness of sexual harassment. You would've thought that talk would have stopped their behavior, but nope, they continued to do it.

One time, Jimmy pinned me down to the ground while Paul proceeded to grind on me in the stairwell. I knew this behavior was inappropriate, but I really liked both guys. I thought one of them would ask me to the school dance, but nope. Both took other girls, and ended up dating those girls. Both girls were light-skinned, biracial girls with more European features and curly hair. I would wonder what was wrong with me that they did not ask me to the dance, or to go "steady." I would look in the mirror and pick myself apart. My hair too short, my skin was too dark, my nose was too wide, and my lips too big — and it did not help that I was being bullied on the school bus, too!

This guy, Nick, who lived up the street from me, would start every morning on the school bus. They had a song called "Bald Head Eagle." I can still hear that song in my head, and that was 31 years ago. The crazy thing about it was that I had medium-length hair and one of the girls who would bully me and sing the song had very short hair, and could not fit it in a ponytail. It would hurt my feelings and make me cry, but I never let them see me cry. I would wait until I got in the house in my room, and I would cry until my head felt like it would explode.

I was starting to get physically sick: headaches, stomachaches, nervousness, and nausea. I think this is when my anxiety started, and I had my first panic attack at that time — not knowing it had a name. I got my bus changed, and I felt better. I used to be nervous Monday through Friday right before going to school. Sometimes, I faked being sick so I would not have to attend school that day, or fake being sick once I got to school so I could get sent home early. The only place I felt safe], protected, and could be myself was at home. The rest of my middle school years were the same, just different years.

When Paul and Jimmy weren't going steady with their girlfriends, they would go back to (I'm going to call it what it was) sexually assaulting me. When they would get back with their girlfriends, they would stop. On the after-school activities bus during my eighth-grade year, Paul asked me for my number, so we exchanged numbers. I remember being happy that this was the first boy who seemed to like me, so I gave my number to him. When I came in from school, I was so excited that I told my dad. My dad said, "Throw that number in the trash; you're still too young to date." So, that was the end of my short-lived happiness as I threw the number away.

Looking back now, I was really messed up to think it was okay to give my number to this boy who never treated me with any respect. I would go many years letting boys/men disrespect me and still mess around with them.

Summer 1994

Before starting high school in the summer of 1994, I would be at my uncle's house in Squirrel Hill. He had just married a much younger woman with three small kids. My mom and my new aunt became close friends. As soon as my mom came home from work, she would change out of her scrubs, and we would visit with them. There was this teenage boy named Robert who lived down the street. He was 18 and very handsome. He stood about 5′ 8″, with clear brown skin, a short haircut, and he dressed nicely. I was 14 at the time, and I had a crush on him. I knew he was older than me, but it didn't matter then.

We became friends, and every time I was at my uncle's house, he would come over to hang out on the porch with me. We would just talk about music and other things teenagers talked about at that time. He was very funny and always made me laugh. He was the first boy to tell me that I was beautiful, and I had my first kiss with him. Hearing someone else besides my parents or family members call me beautiful felt nice. He was supposed to be my boyfriend, so I would call when I got to my uncle's house to let him know I was there.

One time, he asked me to come down to his house. I was 14 and had never gone to a boy's house alone, so I was nervous. I told my little step-cousin Maria, who was five, to come with me since she always followed me around. We went to his house and he told me that the door would already be open, and to come downstairs to the basement. We went down there, and I saw he was lying in his bed. He asked why I brought my cousin with me. I looked at him in a weird way, thinking to myself that I didn't see any reason not to bring her, since all we were going to do was talk like we always did and maybe kiss.

Robert said he wanted to do something else, and I knew what he meant since he had been hinting about having sex lately. I knew I wasn't ready for that, and I wasn't going to let anyone pressure me into having sex. I told him I thought I should leave, so my cousin and I left. We continued talking on the phone and hanging out on my uncle's porch, but I could sense that he just wanted to be my friend.

One day, I went to my uncle's house and hadn't called Robert yet to tell him I was over. I came from around the back of the house, and I stopped dead in my tracks, ran back around to the side of the house, and peeked around the corner. I saw Robert on the other side of the street kissing a girl. The kiss went on for a long time; she was older than me and looked to be more around Robert's age.

This would have been the first time a guy cheated on me. I cried; Robert had broken my heart, and it wouldn't be the last time I felt this way. This situation prepared me for what was to come. I would learn what real pain felt like in a romantic relationship.

High School

It was Fall 1994, and it was time to start high school. My parents did not want my sister and me to attend any "regular" inner-city schools. I had played the clarinet since I was eight, so I auditioned for the School for The Creative and Performing Arts of Pittsburgh (CAPA) and was accepted. You had to have good grades and recommendation letters from two teachers. I was a straight-A student in the National Honors Society and Student of the Month many times. I participated in many school activities, such as band, cheerleading, and track. I also managed the boys' soccer team in middle school.

I was a good girl. I followed the rules so my parents would be proud of me. I liked CAPA; it was a different environment than the one I was used to. You would see a group of guys singing Boyz II Men songs, girls/boys running around with ballet attire on, girls singing Brandy's "I Wanna Be Down," and art students with paint all over their clothes. The best way to describe CAPA was as a real-life Fame (a TV show from the 1980s about a performing arts school).

I was starting to come into myself. The baby weight was coming off, and I had braids like Brandy, the singer. I would put lipstick on once I left the house. I wasn't allowed to wear makeup yet, so I would wait until I was on the school bus or at school. The school was high-pressure and focused on your talent. There were no football or basketball teams, no cheerleading—just your talent. I wanted to attend football games, be a cheerleader, play tennis, and live out that real high school experience, so I decided to leave CAPA.

I ended up at a different high school with two months left of my ninth-grade year. I reconnected with Paul from middle school. I can't recall how, because he went to another high school in the Squirrel Hill area of the city, but he lived close to my school. We started dating, and we would talk on the phone daily. We started talking about having sex. I was a virgin, but he already had experience since the age of 12. I was getting ready to turn 15. I know we shouldn't have been thinking about having sex. At that tender age, I thought this was the love of my life, and I wanted to make him happy.

He used to tell me that I would be his wife one day. We planned for June 15, 1995, the last day of school, to be the day 'it' would happen. I ended up at his house, scared and not knowing what to do. It took a good 20-25 minutes for him to enter me, but it felt like hours when you add in the pain, too. I can seriously say the first time was not good. We did use protection. All through the summer, we would talk, but I told him I did not feel comfortable having sex again. He said okay, but unknown to me, he was okay with it because he was entertaining other girls. Paul ended up transferring schools and also started attending the same school as me.

Our relationship lasted for about two months before he gave me the line. Unfortunately, I would get used to hearing this line many times later in life from other men I dated when they were no longer interested, or after they already had sex with me: "I'm busy," or "I'm not ready for a relationship." If this was true, why have sex with me or act like you wanted a relationship with me when you knew all you wanted was sex? He said being on the football and wrestling teams took up all his time, but he was already on the football and wrestling teams at his previous school when we first started dating. He said it was best if we broke up, but a few weeks later, he was in a relationship with someone else. He wasn't busy; he no longer wanted to give me his time.

I learned throughout life that people would make time for who they want to make time for. No man is too busy to carve out some time to talk, text, or spend time with the woman he loves, unless there's some mental illness or issues that he might be going through, and he needs to figure that out before engaging in a committed relationship. The relationship with this other girl did not last long, because she did not want to have sex with him. That was the rumor that was going around school, and she later confirmed it to be true.

Paul said he wanted to be back with me, so I gave him another chance. We ended up having sex six months later on December 10, 1995. A week later, he told me he was too busy to be in a relationship. That was our last time being in a relationship. We remained friends throughout our teens and 20s, while also having sex a couple of times over the years. In 2007, he was no longer with his girlfriend, whom he had gotten with after the second time he broke up with me. They had been together for 10 years and had been engaged. He thought I would be happy that he was no longer with her and grab him up for myself. Nope, I no longer wanted him like that, and that is when we stopped having sex.

To this day, we're still cordial on social media, and if I run into him, we'll have small talk. However, he's now married to a woman I'm going to introduce later, because we had another guy in common. They have three beautiful kids. He's doing very well in life—many blessings to him and his family.

Shattered

Michael: The First Abuse

I was at school near Christmas time in 1995. Someone took a whole box of candy canes from my teacher's desk in my Spanish class. I knew who the boy was and the class he was in, so my teacher gave me a hall pass to get the box of candy back. As I was walking down the hall, I saw two of the star football players coming through the stairwell. I was in 10th grade, DeShawn was in 11th, and Michael was in 12th. I heard one of them say, "She's pretty. I'm going to get her number." Michael asked me for my number, which I gave him. I was into those light-skinned, curly-haired boys back then, and besides, they were always the ones trying to holla at me. He was 18—and he was fine. He was the star wide receiver on our school's football team. I was flattered that he wanted to get to know me since he had many girls trying to get his attention.

We talked on the phone that night and started dating over winter break. It was a big mistake getting involved with him. He was dating several girls at school, had a main girlfriend who transferred from our school to another school, and was messing with some older woman who lived by his best friend DeShawn's house. We met each other's parents and would hang out at either his or my house. I had no idea he was doing all of this. He was good at hiding all of us naïve girls from one another even though we were in the same school.

I found out he was messing with a girl, Nakisha, who is now Paul's wife and the mother of his three kids. She found out about me, so it became a big problem with us all over this guy. I was never the type to fight over a boy, but this girl and her friends said things to me daily—calling me a whore, hoe, and bitch—all over him. Plus, other girls at the school did not like me. I don't know why, because I never spoke to or had any classes with them.

I was a beautiful girl. I had brown skin and slanted brown eyes. I dressed nicely and carried myself like a classy young lady. I was 5'6, 135 lbs, and built nicely. Most times when I went to the salon, I would wear my hair pulled back into a slick ponytail or a high-fashion bun with waterfall curls. A lot of the boys from ninth to twelfth grade liked me. Even one of the younger security guards would try to shoot his shot at me, too.

Some of those girls at school were jealous, and even called me stuck up and conceited. I can admit that I was feeling myself, but it was confidence—I had high self-esteem. Some girls did not like me because I was comfortable with myself. I loved myself and never cared about what others thought of me. I found that to be the case throughout my adulthood with other women; they would be intimidated by me. I was one of the girls the guys wanted. I ended up being with Michael for 2 1/2 years. He did not treat me well, and most guys treated me poorly throughout the years, too. I never understood why. I was down-to-earth, funny, sweet, caring, non-confrontational, and always supportive of the man I was with. It seemed like they liked those girls who were always fighting, cussing someone out, or hitting on them.

I remember being at Michael's house once. We were watching a show, I think it was Martin. I started laughing, and he punched me so hard in my leg I started to cry. He did this all because I laughed at something funny on TV. Remember, this boy was 18 years old, and I was 16. That was the first time a guy physically abused me, and it would not be the last. He would emotionally and mentally abuse me, too! I don't know where he learned this behavior from, because his stepdad was a very loving man from what I knew and witnessed.

On Valentine's Day, 1996, I went to his house with gifts. I love giving gifts to my loved ones. It's my love language. Back then, I did not know anything about love languages, but I knew I always wanted my family and friends to feel loved and happy. Gifts have a way of showing love. Later in life, this would get people to use me. I got him some silk boxers with hearts on them, a big chocolate candy heart, a pair of Jordans I knew he wanted, and gold stud earrings; the same ones his best friend Deshawn had. Yes, I was 16, treating this boy like a king with my allowance, which my parents gave me to buy myself something. Instead, I used it so he would have a great Valentine's Day.

You all are wondering what he got me, right?

His mom wasn't too thrilled that I got him all those things when she found out all he got me was a plastic rose they were selling at school. She called him upstairs. When he returned, he had a gift bag containing a white teddy bear with a gold necklace around the bear's neck, $50 cash, and a red plastic rose. I should have thanked his mom, because she put that Valentine's Day gift together for me. He could've done better if he wanted to—if he loved me as he said he did. Unknown to his parents and most people, he was selling drugs. I did not know until I saw him with a lot of money, and he told me what he was doing. I was a young, naïve girl, not knowing that people would show you how they felt about you by how they treated you.

My mom threw me a big cookout for my 17th birthday since I did not want a sweet 16 the year before. I thought my boyfriend was going to get me something nice. I never looked for things in return from anyone, because the things I did for others were out of the goodness of my heart — but it was my birthday! He got me an empty birthday card and decided to flirt with other girls at my party. I felt hurt, but I kept that smile on my face like everything was okay. It's the same smile I learned to master over the years to pretend I was good, but I was crying inside and wanted to die most of the time. To this day, I still paint on that pretty face even though I'm crying inside most days.

The most hurtful thing Michael did to me was when he got two separate girls pregnant at the same time. By this time, he had graduated from high school, and was in his second year in college at one of the local state schools playing football. He was in a relationship with me, had two girls pregnant, and was messing around with girls in college, too! Before the babies were born, we knew it was time to end this so-called relationship. He called me in February 1998. He first apologized for how he had treated me.

I remember exactly what he said over the phone: "Rose, I'm sorry for how I treated you. You were a good person to me and was always there for me. I am about to be a father to two little girls, and I would never want anyone to treat my daughters the way I had treated you. I'm sorry. I hope you can forgive me." I cried and told him that I had forgiven him, and told him to do better in the future. The last time I saw Michael was in 2005. I hope he's doing well in life.

Drama and Depression

Throughout my time in high school, I dealt with a lot. In my 11th grade year, I got very sick. I was out of school for a month, and the doctor ordered me to rest. I had a high fever of 102, my stomach felt like someone punched me several times, and it was on fire. My mom took me to the ER. They tested my stomach and listened to it. They diagnosed me right away. The doctor said, "A young girl like yourself should not be this stressed to get gastritis." I had to take this green liquid medication and rest.

My mom would go to the school to pick up my assignments weekly and take back my finished work. I felt so much better after getting away from all the stress and issues at school. When I returned to school, I was shocked that many people had stopped talking to me for unknown reasons and had distanced themselves from me. I felt alone. I always felt alone, but this was the first time I felt like I had no one but my parents.

I know you all are thinking, "You have a sister." Yeah, but she did not like me too much, either. She was even telling people I wasn't her sister. This taught me to depend on myself. My parents were the only ones who were there for me throughout the years. I could not understand what I did to deserve to be treated that way by some people. Some of those girls I thought were my good friends turned out to be pretending to be my friends, and I would find out people would believe anything someone said just to have others like them.

I started wearing black daily. I was depressed, not knowing the name at that time for how I was feeling. I just knew I felt like I no longer wanted to live. I suffered from depression and anxiety several times throughout the years, but never in the traditional way of not wanting to get out of bed, not wanting to go outside, neglecting my responsibilities, etc. I suffered from functional depression.

When I wrote this in January 2022, I was in a very dark, lonely place—a "black hole." A couple of months prior, I had tried to commit suicide, and it wasn't my first time. I had attempted suicide when I was in high school by taking pills. In 2013 I took a whole bottle of pills, and in 2019 I tried to slit my wrist.

I went to Quincy's house on Halloween day in 2021. He was the man I was "dating" whom I loved very much. I remember standing on the top step outside his house and him walking up to me. I gave him a big hug and a lot of pecks of kisses before walking down the steps and saying bye.

He was "pulling away" from me. He did not know it would be the last time he would see me alive. If he had known what I was planning to do, he would not have been so rude to me as I was leaving, ignoring me and taking a call instead.

One of the reasons for me wanting to end my life was the disappointment and hurt of us not being together. Quincy, if you're reading this, don't be angry with me or think it was your fault; this was about me and my mental illness. I sat in my garage on Halloween day 2021, crying so hard that my head started to hurt. I wanted all my pain and all the disappointment I'd gone through to go away. I turned my SUV on, closed my garage door, laid my seat back, and put all the letters I had written on my passenger seat.

I had written letters to my son, my parents, my sister, my son's dad, and the man I was in love with—Quincy. Sitting in my reclined seat, I was ready to meet my maker. The car had been running for about 10 minutes. The only reason I'm still here is that my son called me on FaceTime, which made me think about what I was about to do. My son saved me! I would never want to cause him the pain of knowing that his mom took her own life.

I got a little off track here, but I know you are following along well. I could never lay in bed daily and feel sorry for myself. I got up daily to attend school, work, and hang out. I was counting down the days before graduation. I was so excited to attend my prom.

I had my dad drive me to Sharon, PA, to get the dress I saw in a prom magazine. My dad paid a pretty penny for that dress, too, but my dad did not care about the price of the dress. He was happy that his first-born daughter was graduating from high school and attending her senior prom. I went to prom with Michael's best friend, DeShawn. DeShawn had already graduated high school and was in college playing football for a D1 university. He then played for multiple football teams. Yes, he ended up in the NFL and was a standout.

I had a nice time at my prom, but I was very happy the day I walked across that stage at Soldiers and Sailors Memorial Hall to receive my high school diploma. I thought it would be a fresh start to a new chapter of happiness, but life had other plans for me.

Jamal: The Murder

Jamal was a guy in my neighborhood that I grew up with; he was 22 — and he was fine! He had his pick of any girl he wanted, so I never thought he would want me. On April 9, 1997, my dream came true. I always knew him, but he seemed much older than me. I had a major crush on him, and I found out he was checking me out, too. We exchanged numbers and started talking on the phone. I remember the first time I hung out with him when he drove me home. We talked in the car for a little over an hour, and I remember him telling me how beautiful I was and kissing me.

It was like I floated into the house on a magical cloud. I remember smiling ear to ear. My parents were in the kitchen. My mom was finishing dinner—smothered pork chops, rice, and my favorite: sweet peas. As you can see, that day was special because I remembered what my mom cooked for dinner.

Over the next four years, Jamal and I had a friend-with-benefits relationship. What's the new term, situationship? On August 20, 2000, I told him I loved him for the first time. I asked him how he felt about that. He said, "How could I not love you? We've been messing around for a long time." Even though I was 20, I did not realize this wasn't normal at this age. This man never took me to the movies, a restaurant, or a walk in the park. To think about it, we NEVER went anywhere together outside our neighborhood.

On July 7, 2001, I got a call at 1:30 a.m. from my mom crying and screaming. I was thinking something happened to my dad. I heard her say it was Jamal. My sister and I lived in the same apartment complex at this time. I told my sister that we had to go, it's Jamal! My heart dropped in my stomach when we got down by the playground in our childhood neighborhood. Jamal's black Benz, which was his late dad's (his dad died six months before), was up on a tow truck riddled with bullet holes. I asked a detective a few times if he was dead, and he finally shook his head yes. I lost it! I could not believe he was gone. He was my best friend—a man that I loved.

Years later, two more men that I was once in relationships with would lose their lives as well to gun violence. I have always wanted to know what Jamal needed to talk to me about. He called me 24 hrs before his murder, not knowing I had moved from my parents' house 2 weeks prior.

It's eerie to think the last time I saw him, he was riding past my childhood house, and I was standing outside talking to a male friend. He did not stop; he just looked at me with these sad eyes and waved. It's like a black cloud followed his car. I never thought that would be the last time I saw him alive.

I know he wanted the best for me and always told me to do well in school. I hope you're proud of me, Jamal — I did it! I graduated college with two degrees with honors!

Malik & Tre: The Date Rape

I first met Rashad in the wintertime of 1996. I was leaving school, and he was walking past. He stopped me and asked for my number. I was with Michael, but I knew he was up at college cheating. Rashad and I talked on the phone for about two months but lost contact.

Fast forward to Spring 1999, I was getting donuts, and as I was coming out of the donut shop, this silver Lexus with tinted windows rolled into the parking lot. All I heard was, "Hey, you with the box of donuts, hold up." The guy exited the car, and I looked at him like I knew I knew him from somewhere. We exchanged numbers, and I realized who he was! He was now going by a different name: Malik. That night, he called me, and I asked him if he remembered me. He said yeah, I do remember you now. We ended up talking until the following morning.

Malik explained to me that he got locked up and had been out for a year. He told me upfront that he was still in the "game." I never was the one to judge a man for how he made a living. In my 20s, I would date men who were drug dealers in corporate America, NFL players, and police officers. I thank him for being honest with me. He would take me to eat, to the movies, or sometimes to both. I would go over to the apartment that he shared with his roommate Tre, but when I would be over, Tre usually wasn't there. I met Tre about three times, but something about his vibe wasn't right.

One night, Malik asked if I wanted to come over to watch a movie. I asked him if his roommate would be there. He said no, so I said okay. I did not feel comfortable being there when Tre was there. Malik and I were chilling, and we started kissing. He started undressing me, and out of nowhere, Tre was standing there. I was trying to tell Malik to stop because Tre was standing there. As I was saying this, Malik said, "I know," with a smirk. That's when I was like, nope, it's not going to happen; as I was trying to get up, Malik pushed me back down onto the couch and held me down. He forced himself into me, and Tre was attempting to put his penis in my mouth. I would not open my mouth, so he smacked me hard in my face and said, "Open your mouth, and if you bite me, I'll kill you."

They took turns having sex with me. I was crying and asking them to let me go. They ignored my cries. They raped me close to two hours, and it seemed like forever. Malik told me to put my clothes on, and I better not tell anyone. He dropped me off at home. I'm glad my parents were asleep. I went to my room soft crying, stripped off my clothes, and got in a hot shower. Thank goodness they did use condoms. I felt dirty, and I blamed myself for being stupid to go over to watch a movie. When asked what happened to my face, I lied and said I slipped and fell.

Malik called me about a week later and asked if I wanted to hang out. I cussed him out, and he laughed and said "I got what I wanted anyway." A couple of years later, I found out he was talking to a girl I knew and tried the same thing with her. Some other guy was already sitting there, so she lied about having to grab something out of her car. She went to her car and drove off; she knew something wasn't right.

I knew they had done this before, and I would not be surprised if they had done this many times after what they had done to me. I never saw Tre again. I don't believe he was from Pittsburgh. He stayed with Malik to attend school, but now I think that might have been a lie. As for Malik, I last saw him riding past me as I was in the car with Donell, my boyfriend, in 2005. I hope Malik is not still preying on young girls.

Donell: Domestic Violence

I met Donell in September 1999. I was 19, he was 29, and he looked like one of my favorite R&B singers. We talked for almost two hours out in front of my parents' house. We had a lot in common, and we exchanged numbers. After talking for weeks, he told me that his aunt, whom he lived with, was going out of town, and he wanted me to spend the weekend with him, so I did. We had a nice weekend going to dinner and the movies. We started dating and Donell introduced me to his mother, so I thought all was good. Come to find out, the woman who I thought was his aunt was really his woman. He tried telling me he was no longer with her and was just staying there.

I told him that it was over. Within a week, he called me to let me know he moved out of that home. We got back together, and on Christmas Day 1999, he proposed to me with a beautiful diamond ring, and I said yes. This would also be the first time he physically abused me. I was 19, still living at my parents' home. We argued in my bedroom, and he asked for his ring back. As I gave him the ring back, it fell on the floor. I bent down to pick it up, and he stomped on my fingers with his sized 11 Timberland boot. I was shocked that he did that to me, and my cry was stuck in my throat. Then he smacked me in my face. I told him to get out of my parents' home. He called me apologizing and said he would never do that again, so I took him back a few days later.

On June 18, 2001, we moved in together. This was when I started to see his true colors. It was a very nice apartment, and he purchased everything I picked out. Things were going well with us, and he hadn't put his hands on me again. That would soon come to an end.

Remember I told you my best friend was murdered on July 7th? Losing Jamal was one of the most challenging days of my life. He wasn't just my best friend; I loved this man, and he was always a phone call away. I went down to the crime scene by my childhood house. I called my friend Johnny and told him what happened. He came right away. He knew I needed that support, and he knew how I felt about Jamal.

Donell came and told me to get in the car to go home. I thought he was concerned about me and wanted to ensure I was good—at least, that's how he made it seem in front of my mom and Johnny. Once we got up the street, he stopped the car, grabbed me by my hair and slammed the side of my head into the passenger side window, smacked me, and said, "I don't give a fuck about that nigga getting killed, why you down there talking to some nigga for?" I could not answer because, once again, my cry was stuck in my throat, and I could not believe he just did that to me.

We got home, and he acted as if nothing had happened. I stayed up for the rest of the night, sitting in the living room with the TV on but not watching it. I was so numb from learning that Jamal, a person that I would confide in, was gone, and this man who claimed to love me had just physically abused me. This man was crazy because he really showed up at Jamal's viewing. I never would understand what for.

Over the years, there was more abuse, lies, cheating, and coming home all times of the night, or sometimes, not at all. This man even destroyed some of my property, like clothes and other items. One time, I came home to find some of my clothes laid out on my bed cut up, and another time, I came home to a knife stabbed through a basketball I just purchased on the living room floor. This was all because I went to my parents' house, and he thought I was cheating. He would do drive-bys to ensure I was at my parents' house when I visited them. Once, he parked up the street, and as I was leaving, he came driving down the street, pretending to be coming from his mom's house because he thought he had left his wallet there.

I decided to throw him a romantic 33rd birthday party. His birthday was at the end of May. It was a beautiful day, and I was cooking out. He decided to get some drinks with his friends at the bar. I told him to make sure to come home around 7 p.m. At this time, we lived on a quiet cul-de-sac street. I made a few runs to pick up the cake, grabbed some outfits at the mall, and decorated the house with balloons and a Happy Birthday banner. I cooked the food, everything was in place, and I wrapped the presents.

I paged him at 8 p.m. since he hadn't come home yet. I did not get a callback. I called his mom, but he wasn't over there. I called his one cousin; he wasn't over there either. It was midnight, and there was still no Donell. This man came rolling into the house around 4 a.m. I was sleeping on the couch when he came in. I asked him what had happened and if he had forgotten about his birthday. He said he was at his mom's and fell asleep. I told him I called there, and his mom said he came past around 2 p.m and left shortly after. He said, "I'm grown. I do what I want to do. Don't question me about my whereabouts."

I did not feel like having a confrontation with him, so I got up from the dining room table where I was sitting to go to bed. He came over and pushed me to the floor. He then picked up one of the dining room wooden chairs and smashed it over my body. The chair crumbled into pieces, and I was in shock. My body felt like it was on fire.

I tried to get up, and he pushed me back down to the floor again and punched me so hard in my back that I felt it in my stomach. He left me there crying and hurt while he went to take a shower. After his shower, he stepped over me and got himself together for bed. I was able to get up after an hour; I was hurting all over. I couldn't sit for almost a week, so I had to call off from work. I worked at a bank as a loan officer, and sitting at my desk for my eight-hour shift was a requirement. I could only lay on my side. I never got an apology or anything.

One time, he pushed me so hard that I fell through the living room coffee table. I covered my face so that the flying glass would not cut me. He grabbed a kitchen knife and cut me right in between my forearm. I have a 3/4-inch scare there to this day. I forgot why he got so mad that day. I even fractured my foot running from him because he was beating on me. I was on crutches for two weeks. He pretended that did not happen, too. The really crazy stuff started happening at the end of our relationship.

Early in our relationship, a male friend of my sister told me that Donell messed around with men. Of course, I confronted him about this, and he told me it was a lie. I can recall two incidents that were super-duper red flags that he was messing with men. Once, a white guy named Danny, who used to work at a "sex store" downtown, called for Donell. I asked Danny why he was calling. He said that they were friends, and he had just returned from Vegas and had a couple of gifts to give Donell. Strange!

Donell returned home with a Vegas T-shirt, shot glasses, candy, and $500. I was confused about why this man would give him all this stuff. He said that he and Danny went way back and had helped him out in the past. I said OK. Danny never called the house again, and I never heard anything about that man since that day. The second incident was when I went to my uncle's wife's house, and she had her nephew James staying there. James was openly gay, and I am sad to say that James got killed in 2005 at a local bar by a security guard.

I introduced James to Donell, and they said hello. We stayed for about an hour and left. I got a call from my aunt later that night saying, "James said he knows Donell, and that he's gay." I was shocked and asked my aunt how James knew this. She said, "Because James has been with him." You could call me stupid, dumb, or super in love, but I did not believe it and dismissed the whole conversation. All of it was true! He was a DL (Down Low) brother!

He also lied about how many kids he had. When I met him, he said he had two kids, a boy and a girl. I ended up meeting both; we would go to the movies and out to eat. His son had to come live with us in 2013 when his mom passed away unexpectedly at 31 years of age. They never determined the cause of death, but they thought her boyfriend had something to do with it, but they could not prove it.

One day, I came home to a large yellow envelope on the porch with his name on it. I saw that it was from the family court division. There were rumors that he had fathered a couple of kids while we were together. I went through the papers and could not believe my eyes. All the kids were born before he and I were together, but there were seven kids by seven different women. Even with the evidence in hand and DNA testing all 99.99%, he still said the kids weren't his.

After finding out about the other kids, I came home from work one day, and all his belongings were gone. He never showed up at home that night. The next morning, he found himself a new woman and moved in with her and her three kids in Section 8 housing. He purchased cell phones for them, and the bill came to our house by accident. I called the number and spoke to the woman. Donell told this lady I was his cousin, that I had nowhere to go, so he let me live in his house until I could make other arrangements.

One night in October 2005, he called me saying he was going to jump off a bridge. I told him if he really was going to commit suicide, he wouldn't have called me; he would have done it, and I hung up on him. He called back, asking if he could come to the house. I told him I did not care what he did. He came to the house. That's when I found out this lady threw him out because her kid's dad had just come home from jail and was going to be paroled at her house. Donell was home for two weeks. Again, I came home to discover all his belongings were gone. She kicked her kid's dad out and told Donell to come back, and he went. I lived alone in our home for about a year and decided to move back home with my parents until I made other arrangements.

In 2015, eight years after we parted ways, I had a brief conversation with Donell. He told me the truth. He was bisexual, and he apologized to me. I haven't kept in regular touch with Donell, but we have talked a couple of times over the years on the phone and on social media, and the last time I saw him in person was in 2017 at a grocery store. I forgave him in 2015 when we had that conversation about him being bisexual. I had to do that for myself to be able to have healing, peace, and closure from that relationship.

I wish him well in life.

Vince: The Rebound

In 2004, I cheated on Donell with Vince since Donell was cheating on me. I know two wrongs don't make it right. I met Vince on a phone chat line. Vince and I had gone to the same high school, but he was three years younger than me. I could not remember him, but he remembered me. Vince was my peace away from the craziness of being in a relationship with Donell. Donell was out there cheating, not coming home, and lying. I did not feel bad about messing with Vince.

He was nice. He was in college, majoring in criminal justice, working for a youth detention center as a youth correction officer, and had a brand-new SUV. He did live at home with his mom and two sisters. He was most definitely a mama's boy. He spent all his quality time mainly with his mom and sisters, but he would invite me over on Mondays for Monday Night Raw WWE and cook for me. I did not realize this was a rebound relationship at that time.

After parting ways with Donell, Vince and I kept doing all the things we were doing when I was cheating with him: movies, walks in the park, sex, and going out to eat. Vince and I never argued, but he sometimes said mean things to me before we became exclusive. One time, he told me that I looked better in my license picture than in person because I looked lighter on my license. One time, I told him something in private, and he threw it back up in my face when he got angry with me. Those were red flags that I ignored.

After we were in a relationship, he didn't insult me any longer, but he did choke me one time. It's so strange how I forgot about that incident. It's like I blocked it out. I remember he did it because he thought that's what I wanted, and that it would make me love him like I did when I was with Donell. That was very confusing, and it's still confusing to me. Why would I love him like I did Donell when he was abusive to me? We enjoyed each other's company, and he adored me. He would tell me that I was beautiful and that he really loved me, and he showed it through his actions. Everything was going well. We started talking about marriage and kids.

His mom was rushed to the hospital ER a week prior because she wasn't feeling well. Then, April 3, 2006 happened; it was unexpected and sad. What they thought to be the common cold was something else, but they did not know what. Her organs started to shut down, and they had to put her in a medically induced coma. The doctors said it did not look good, but we kept the faith that she'd pull through. Vince and I went to the church to light a candle and to pray. Sadly, on April 3, 2006, she passed away from SARS, now known as COVID-19.

Vince took his mom's passing very hard, being that he loved his mom so much. I was there for him the best way I knew how, but he would lash out at me and his sisters.

He broke up with me unexpectedly on my 27th birthday, June 22, 2007. The crazy thing was that we were looking at engagement rings two weeks prior. I was sad, but it was a relief since I no longer had to walk around on eggshells around him. I was not allowed to mention anything about my mom around him. That was a demand he made, and out of respect, I did not mention my mom around him. For example, if I had dinner with my mom, I would lie and say I went with my dad or sister. The relationship became exhausting!

By this time, I had become friends with a man named Raymond, and he was a piece of work, too! I will introduce him later. Vince found out about Raymond because he had purchased a cell phone for me and had paid the bill. He looked through the call logs to see who I was talking to. Vince called Raymond, and they had words, but I did not understand why he was so angry at that time—he was the one who left me! I gave him that phone back and got my own phone plan.

Vince was so angry with me that he would call my house saying he was going to get girls to come to my job or home to fight me. He would call me nasty names, say rude things about me, and even threaten to release some sexy pictures to social media that I sent him. I blocked his number and told him to stop driving past my parents' house.

I met this guy, Bill, off Myspace. After our second date, I learned he worked as a youth correction officer with Vince at the youth detention center. What a small world! Vince found out that Bill was talking to me, and tried to fight him at work. He also tried to run him off the road. Bill left me alone after that! Vince was 6'4 and 240 lbs then, and Bill was way smaller than him.

Vince and I kept in contact, and would still hook up from time to time. Why would I still hook up with someone who threatened to get me beat up and release sexy pictures of me on social media?

On August 30, 2008, he came to my house to see me. He lay across my bed and started to cry. I thought it was him feeling sad about his mom. I hugged him and rubbed his back, letting him know I was there for him, and that everything would be okay. He said, "I'm so sorry, Rose." As soon as he made that statement, my stomach started to hurt, and my mind started to race back to a dream I had a couple of days ago. I asked, "Did you get someone pregnant?" He looked at me and said yes. I asked if it was his coworker we had seen three years prior.

He said yes.

I knew something was going on with them then. He tried to tell me he never messed with her or any other woman while we were together, but I knew that was a lie. We were at a pizza shop in Monroeville, and he said, "There's my coworker." She did not speak, nor did he speak, but something in my gut told me something was going on with them. He welcomed his son into the world in November 2008. That night, he came to my house to show me the camcorder tape of the baby being born. I said, "Please go and be with your family." This man was goofy. He told me he was going to take his son, and we were going to get married and raise him together. I looked at him like he was crazy.

I stopped communicating with Vince after that. I spoke to him in March 2010. He was talking about trying again with me, but I said no. I had met a new guy, and I wanted to see what could happen with him. I did not see Vince again until September 2021 at his dad's funeral.

He's doing well and engaged; his son is a very handsome teenager. I wish him and his family the best.

Rose

After cutting all ties with Vince in 2008, I decided to be alone and to be celibate. I decided to be celibate because I no longer wanted to have sex with men who were going to waste my time. Men that weren't aligned with my values did not deserve access to me.

Ladies, we should treat our bodies as the beautiful temples they are. Every man doesn't deserve access to us.

I was also in college finishing up my second degree. During the week, I worked at the bank and attended school on Saturdays from 8 a.m. to 5 p.m. in the Adult Accelerated Course at Point Park University (PPU). I did not want to date, but a year prior, in August 2007, I met Raymond on Myspace. That platform was very popular at the time. He was 29 years old—6'1", 215 lbs, muscular, with dark black wavy hair, thick eyebrows, full lips, and a light complexion. Raymond was fine, and he knew it. He had a lot of women that wanted his attention.

He left me a message in my DMs asking for my number. I gave him my number, and within minutes, he called me! We talked on the phone for about an hour, getting to know one another and asking the basic questions. Raymond wanted to meet me that night, so I said sure since I wasn't doing anything then, and I was single. The first thing he said to me when he saw me was, "Your pictures don't do you justice; you're beautiful!" I have heard that pictures do not showcase my true beauty a few times before. This man was straightforward. He wasn't playing any games or wasting any time. He grabbed me in his arms and kissed me. I was shocked! That never happened to me before and has never happened since.

He asked, "Are you coming with me tonight?" I was single, he was fine, and I liked how he wasn't afraid to be himself; but I had to decline his invitation. I was on a journey of celibacy, and I wasn't going to let a nice-looking man steer me off course. Raymond was college-educated and had a great job as a case manager in the court system, but he was a male exotic dancer on the weekends.

Yes, you read that right.

The funny thing was that when he told me his stage name, I had never heard of him before, and he was one of the best in the city. After that day, he would call me daily, and we would talk for hours. At that time, he wanted more, but I was cautious because he was an attractive man with a profession involving many women. I did not want this man to break my heart. I was exhausted from the pain I had already endured from my previous relationships. It was best for us to be platonic friends. It was nice to have a male friend with whom I could hang out without all the added pressure of a relationship.

When I wasn't hanging out with Raymond, I started my event planning business, Elegant Impressions. I planned weddings, birthday parties, and other events. I ran into DeShawn, my prom date, who ended up in the NFL. We exchanged numbers to catch up, and I told him about my event planning business. He put me in touch with his agent, Doug, from Philly. From there, I started working with a marketing company based in Atlanta that did events for high-profile sports athletes.

Raymond ended up in a medical crisis, and when I wasn't working, at school, or working on my business, I would run small errands for him and bring him dinner. Also, since he was bed bound, he wanted company. I would sit with him for a few hours talking, really getting to know one another better. We always had good conversations, mostly about life and the things we wanted to do. After he was able to move around again, I started to see less of him. I knew it had a lot to do with me being celibate.

When you decide to be celibate and set boundaries for yourself, you're going to lose those men who once found you attractive. They found you attractive but looked at you as more of an object. I learned the difference between someone finding you attractive and being interested in you. I found out he was seeing many different women. Then, I called him one day, but his number was disconnected. I went past his house; it looked vacant. He stopped posting on all of his social media sites. I was sad and hurt that someone I considered a good friend would just up and leave without saying anything.

It was the summer of 2009. I went on finishing up with school and doing these events for some of the big-name NFL players in the city. I decided to take my summer classes online to have enough time to make a name for myself in the event planning industry. I did a couple of mini camps, players' kids' birthday parties, and other events for different players. I started hanging around in that circle. I'd be at some club in the city up in V.I.P., seeing things I did not know went on in that circle—a lot of sex, alcohol, and drugs. I stayed true to myself and knew when it was my time to leave.

I made some new friends and a lot of money that summer, but it was time to return to school for my last fall term. I was almost at the finish line! I was very focused on writing papers and putting the finishing touches on my big group presentation. I was still riding solo and celibate. I'm not going to lie; there were times I was lonely, but I was at peace. I would rather be lonely than lie with a man I wasn't in love with. Sex is mental for me. I have to feel emotionally connected and safe with that man to experience sexual desire and pleasure.

December 13, 2009, was my last day at PPU. After I gave my presentation, it was a done deal. That night, I went out to celebrate with some friends at a lounge. About a week later, Raymond finally posted a picture of himself with this beautiful older woman on his social media platform with the caption "Mr. & Mrs. Smith." This man had moved to Arizona and married a woman he had met off social media after talking on the phone for four months.

We ended up having a phone conversation. Raymond said he married her because I did not want more with him. He apologized for leaving without saying anything. At that time, I no longer wanted to be friends with him. I had just started talking to a nice guy named Tristan, whom I had met on a black dating site. Raymond and I wished each other well and went our separate ways.

I did run into him years later at a furniture store. He was with his new fiancée, and I was with my fiancé Tristan. We introduced our partners to one another, had small talk, and said our farewells. I hope all is well with him.

Too Good to Be True

Tristan

By January 2010, I had met a nice guy on a dating site for Black singles. It's wild because I left him a message in December 2009, but he never got back to me, so I took it as he wasn't interested.

On Saturday morning, January 9, 2010, the last day of my membership (I wasn't going to renew), he sent me a message and asked if we could send direct messages. We messaged back and forth for two hours, and he asked for my number, and I gave it to him. From that day on, we never stopped talking. Tristan was different from the other guys I had dated. He was educated, pleasant, polite, respectful, and handsome. At 27, he was doing well for himself. He told me he had just ended a long-term relationship with his college girlfriend and moved into his condo.

He had a good corporate job as a computer programmer/coder for a top insurance company in Pittsburgh. He drove a new Mercedes Benz, had good credit, and had a 401k. He was, and still is the only person I know who faithfully paid his student loans every month until they were paid in full. At first, I thought he was too good to be true, but in October 2009, I wrote down what I wanted in a man and prayed nightly to God for that man. God gave me everything I wanted and more in Tristan.

After a couple of days of talking, I fainted at home and had to get rushed to the ER. I was bleeding vaginally for three months straight. My blood count was very low. They admitted me into the hospital, and I had to have two blood transfusions. I was in the hospital for three days. Tristan texted me to check on me. I was shocked because I had only talked to him for about four days before this happened, and he was really concerned about me. I made a mental note of that kind gesture.

After I left the hospital, we made plans to meet soon after. When I was discharged from the hospital Friday night, Tristan went out with his friends. He asked if it was okay if he called when he got in, and I said sure. I thought this man was not calling me when he got in, and to my surprise, he texted me at 2:30 a.m. to see if I was still up. We ended up texting until 6 a.m. I knew from that moment that this man was different.

On January 17, 2010, we texted all day. At 1:30 a.m., he asked if I wanted to come over. I thought to myself, this was booty-call hours. I said sure. I got up, took a shower, and put on some clothes. I came with an overnight bag. I changed into my pajamas right in front of him. It was cute that he was a little shy about me doing that. We stayed up talking for a couple of hours. Tristan told me to take the bed, and he would sleep on the couch. I was shocked. I told him that I had no problems sleeping in the bed with him. To be truthful, I wanted to cuddle because it had been too long since I laid in bed with a man I liked, or any man at all at that time. We did fool around a little that night, but we did not have sex.

I started spending every weekend at his place. Friday, after he came home from work, he would come to get me, and I would not leave until Sunday before the football games came on. He's a huge Steelers fan! From the beginning, I knew this man was into me and wanted me to be a part of his life long-term. Within a month, I met all his close friends, and we hung out a few times with them and their wives or girlfriends.

We first said "I love you" on April 25, 2010, while showering together. We had just come in from an NFL draft party that I had been invited to by a friend who was an NFL agent. I was doing event planning for NFL players, and was running around in that circle at that time. I said, "I love you," and he quickly said it back. We made it official on June 7, 2010.

Tristan did it up for my 30th birthday! We did a bike ride trail, and I ended up becoming overheated. I suffer from iron deficiency anemia and passed out on the railroad tracks in Oakland. I was okay after getting fluids into my system. I busted open my left knee, and I still have that scar to this day. I did not let that put a damper on the beautiful weekend he had planned for me. He took me to the Spaghetti Warehouse for dinner (it used to be one of my favorite restaurants) and to a nightclub afterward. He also took me to Put in Bay, Ohio, for a weekend getaway. He's the only guy who ever did something that nice for me, and he's the only man I dated who I vacationed with. We went out of the country on several vacations over the years.

He took me to his hometown to meet his parents and younger sisters for a Labor Day cookout. Tristan had asked me a couple of times to move in with him, but I wanted to live on my own since I had already lived with my ex-fiancé. I did not want to live with a man again unless I knew he could potentially be my husband. At that time, I started dating with a purpose. I knew what I wanted and did not want.

My dad is a firm believer that you really don't know someone until you live with them, and that was always in the back of my head. So, I moved in with him on August 28, 2010, seven months after meeting. Like I said, this man knew he wanted to be with me. It should not take years for a man to know if he wants you in his life long-term. It was good, and we had a great time getting to know one another better and enjoying each other's company. We would talk about our future together all the time. Tristan knew he wanted me as his wife and the mother of his kids. He was never on the fence about me or unsure. Tristan was an emotionally available man. He knew what I brought to the table, and he knew I was a good woman— someone he could see himself building a life with.

We wanted to travel and enjoy being a couple without kids for a couple of years. Well, it did not turn out the way we planned it. I would fall asleep daily at 5 pm. We thought I was coming down with something. I missed my period, but they were irregular anyway. I told him I thought I was pregnant. He came home the next day from work with an EPT test. I went into the bathroom to pee on the stick; I did not need to wait for the recommended 2 minutes. As soon as I started to pee on the stick, the word pregnant appeared instantly on the screen. I screamed, "Tristan, I'm pregnant!"

He looked at the instructions, then at the stick, and then back at the instructions. He said to take the other one in the morning. They said the pregnancy hormones would be higher in the morning. I just laughed because he was either shocked, or in denial. I took the other test in the morning, and he still did not believe I was pregnant. I made a doctor's appointment, and they came in and said," Congratulations, Ms. Harris, you're pregnant!" I called Tristan. He was still at work in his office. He said, "I'm glad I'm still sitting down, or I would have passed out." He was shocked, but happy—we were having a baby!

Our son Henry was born July 5, 2011, three weeks before my due date of July 28, 2011, but he was healthy and beautiful. He had the same slanted eyes as me, dimples, and a full head of silky black hair.

We were thrilled to be first-time parents. I was delighted to be a mom, and was a natural at it. I stayed home with our son, and Tristan provided for us. Tristan is an amazing man and dad. I could not have asked for a better man to have a child with. I ensured I took care of everything, including the household chores and our son. All Tristan had to do was provide for his family. I always wanted things to be stress-free for him because I believe Black men have it hard daily just being Black in America. The last place they should feel defeated or unloved was in their own home with their woman.

Homeowners

Our son was turning two, and we did not want to raise him in a condo, so it was time to look for a house!

We found our home in the east suburbs of Pittsburgh on a quiet cul-de-sac street. We signed the papers on December 13, 2013. At that time, I had just started working for one of the biggest hospitals in Pittsburgh. I was in patient support, a full time mom, decorating our new house, cleaning, cooking, laundry, and sex. You name it, I did it. Sometimes, I didn't know how I made it through the week. Tristan would help by cooking some nights, and picking me up from work.

At that time, he had started a new corporate job and became distant from me. I did not know what was going on. We had been together for almost four years and had already been engaged for a year. We would have our share of disagreements, and he felt I was trying to be his "mom" at times, but I'm a nurturer to the core. What he thought was me trying to be his "mom" was being an overprotective and overly loving woman to her man.

We got through that rough patch, and still to this day, I don't know what was going on at that time.

I suspected that he might've been emotionally cheating on me with someone because he was talking to women on dating sites. I did a Google search of his name. A new dating site profile popped up for him, and he was chatting with a couple of women. He deleted the profile in front of me once I confronted him about it.

Over the years, there would be more issues with distance from him. I experienced the same with another man I became involved with, too.

***

Digital Download, LLC.

By this time, it was January 2016, and Tristan had already suspected for six months that he would be fired from his corporate job. This white lady who was a project manager on his team in another state just seemed to have it out for him.

This situation wasn't the first time he had dealt with issues like this in corporate America. He would usually be the only Black person and the youngest on a team of all white people. On top of that, he made six figures and had nice incentives for working for this company. He had a side hustle doing ads for clients on a social media site, bringing in an extra monthly income. He was preparing for the day his corporate job fired him. He always wanted to ensure he could provide for our family, as we had a mortgage and other bills to pay. Also, we wanted to have great insurance since our son had an articulation and pronunciation disability and would have speech sessions at a local children's hospital. I believed that our son had ADHD or a mild form of Autism, but the doctors never wanted to diagnose him with either. Our son always met his milestones on time and performed well in school.

Tristan was under a lot of stress and he began having stomach issues. I always made sure to take care of everything, so all he had to do was focus on work and his side hustle. I would do nice gestures for him by buying him small gifts or making his favorite food. I would always uplift and support him. I was his number-one cheerleader! I learned so much from my mom, but one thing I learned by watching her was how to take care of my man. She always supported my dad's goals and dreams, no matter what or how crazy they may have seemed at the time. I always ensured I did that with the men I was in a relationship with and my male friends.

January 13, 2016 was "doomed day!" The big boss from New York was coming into the office that day. They had Tristan's team go to a conference room but asked Tristian to accompany them to his manager's office. He texted me that they fired him, and asked for me to come pick him up. He rode the bus daily into town, and had to bring home a few more items. He knew he would be fired, so he would bring things home from his office daily, like drawings Henry made for him, a small heater, and snacks. I was surprised he was calm and happy.

I guess he no longer had to play this waiting game of when they would ax him, and I knew he was under a great deal of stress that I knew had to decrease. As soon as he got into the house, he went into our home office, and his side hustle became his main hustle! Tristan would spend hours in his office building his company, Digital Download, LLC. He would try to come out to eat dinner with our son and me or watch a show with me, but he would usually be in the office. He always made it a priority to play with our son for at least an hour a day.

I preferred our son got his attention rather than have Tristan trying to divide up that time between our son and me. I had to be strong and keep my emotions in check. Tristan's business took off fast, and we saw major growth monthly. I would help Tristan out with the business, and I was his first employee. I would manually do the clients' reports every Sunday and do other small tasks for the business. Within almost a year, Tristan was able to hire a couple of full-time employees and lease an office inside an office building. At the five-year mark, Digital Download, LLC was a major black-owned digital marketing firm with many top clients!

Tristan became an entrepreneur, an author, a business motivational speaker, and a business coach. He held many workshops and mastermind seminars for new start-up business owners. He took Digital Download, LLC from a zero to over a seven-figure agency within three years.

You know how they say, "With more money comes more problems?" Tristian started to run in a circle with a lot of people who were millionaires. One of the most prominent digital marketers in the US flew him out to Seattle, Washington, to hang out with others in the industry. They all stayed at this digital marketer mogul's cabin and partied on his yacht.

By hanging out with these people, he started to learn about different organic remedies and other things wealthy people would use or do to improve brain function, etc. We bumped heads one night because I told him to research before taking, or trying things he had never heard of.

He proceeded to tell me that we did not have a connection and that he would never marry me. I was shocked he said all that just because I had told him to do his research on some of the remedies he had never heard about.

Tristan proposed to me on February 18, 2013. We had been engaged for 7 years and together for 10 years, but never married. Him telling me that he would never marry me hurt me to the core, but I stayed to make it work for our son, and I still loved him. By May 2018, he had one foot inside our home, and another out the front door. He was considering getting an apartment while our son and I would continue living in the house.

This man told me he did not like me, and that we wouldn't even be friends if he didn't know me. By this time, I was slowly falling out of love with Tristan, but we were both content, so we stayed in the relationship. There were nights when I would lay next to the man I had a child with—the man I was engaged to, the man I thought I would spend the rest of my life with—and cry because I was hurt, sad, and unhappy. I just wanted to be respected, cherished, and loved!

2019 Quincy: My Blessing?

By March 2019, I started therapy for anger management, not realizing I needed treatment for way more than anger management. There was a genuine reason for my anger, and it wasn't just about sitting in the car rider's line at my son's school Monday-Friday, the crazy drivers on the road, Tristan, or our relationship. God decided to put someone in my life to make me realize what I needed to be working on.

I met Quincy In 1998 when I was 17, and he was 18. He had just moved to Pittsburgh from another city, and I was friends with his cousin. I thought Quincy was fine, but I was talking to his cousin, so I quickly put that thought about getting to know him better out of my head. Over the years, I would think about him and wonder how he was doing, so I was happy when we became social media friends. Over the years, we would say hi or like one another's posts or pictures; nothing was out of the norm.

In October 2018, I visited his page more often, and he would post some funny things. I was very unhappy and sad, so by going to his page, I knew I would get a good laugh, and it was never a disappointment. I started to feel something for him. It was like a force drawing me to him, or maybe it was all in my head. So, when he DM'd me asking if he could take me on a "coffee date," I accepted his invitation.

We met at a popular coffee shop on May 18, 2019. I did not know that would be the day my life would change forever. I could sense that he was happy to see me, and I was happy to see him as well and wanted to catch up. He came dressed to impress. Quincy had on a pair of blue slacks, a button-up shirt, a blue vest, and some nice brown dress boots. He smelled good when he hugged me. I later found out he was wearing Dior Sauvage. I always loved a man who dressed nice and smelled good.

He had already ordered my green tea lemonade. It's my favorite drink and the only thing I would usually get from this coffee house. My time was limited since Henry had a recital that day. I was instantly comfortable with him. Maybe because we had spent time around one another—but that was 21 years ago. I had an instant divine connection with Quincy.

We sat outside on a lovely Spring morning. He made me laugh, and I was amazed at how handsome he had become with age. We said our goodbyes after about an hour, but I wanted to stay and continue our conversation. I just wanted to be in his presence. I could sense that he wasn't ready for me to leave, either. I fell in love with him that day. Over the next few weeks, we would text here and there to say hello. On June 28th, I texted Quincy since Tristan had gone out with his friends to do ax throwing for his one boy's birthday.

Quincy was happy to hear from me and wanted me to meet up with him, but I let him know that Tristan wasn't home and my son was in bed, so we talked on the phone. Out of the clear blue, Quincy said, "Rose, what are your demons?" At first, I was puzzled by his question, but then my answer came to mind, and this would be my first time speaking this to anyone. I told him when I was younger, a female cousin molested me.

He didn't reply for what felt like hours, but he responded and said, "Wow, do you want to talk about it?" I proceeded by telling him what happened. I felt I could confide in him, which I hadn't been able to do in years because I thought I had to be perfect with Tristan, and Tristan wasn't an affectionate person. Most of the time, when I would talk, he would ignore me.

Quincy and I planned to meet the next day for coffee or drinks. Many did not know that the supermarket in Fox Chapel had a bar in the back. I text him so we could meet for drinks, and we sat at the bar catching up. Since I had to be at my son's recital the last time we were together, we were able to sit and talk without a time limit. This time, he revealed some things going on in his life, and I was open with him about things going on in my life, too. It was so easy to talk to him. We talked for about three hours. I walked out to his car afterwards, but I was returning after our goodbyes to do some grocery shopping.

Again, I did not want to say goodbye to him. We hugged, but it was a little longer and tighter this time, and it felt right to be in his arms. I pulled back and looked at him. I wanted him to kiss me, but we did not kiss. While grocery shopping, I could not get him off my mind, but I also thought about Tristan. I firmly believe that everything happens for a reason, that our lives have already been written, and that we're just playing it out in real time.

Quincy told me to text him to make sure I got home okay. I did that as soon as I got in, and I started putting the groceries away to begin preparing dinner for Tristan and Henry. Quincy texted me back, saying he was glad I made it home okay and wanted to tell me something. I asked what, but he said he did not want to tell me, but I convinced him that he could tell me anything. I wasn't quite prepared for what Quincy would text me next. I knew he was attracted to me even though he thought I did not know. I sometimes play naïve, but I be knowing!

He texted that he wanted to give me oral sex. I was speechless, so I sent him the big eye emoji. He quickly apologized to me for being so forthcoming, but I told him that it was okay because, to tell you the truth, I already felt the sexual connection between us.

We talked about him working out with me at the park the next day. I texted him mid-morning asking if he wanted to work out with me, and that I would head to the park soon to walk/jog. He said he was day drinking; I was confused because I had never heard of day drinking. He told me what it was and asked if I wanted to join him, so I said, "Sure, text me your address."

He did not live too far from me. When I got to his house, he hugged me tightly. He made us some mimosas, and we listened to music and talked about when we were teenagers and our lives now. He told me he wanted to do a lot of good things to help people, and make a significant impact one day by being a speaker. I had been at his house for about five hours. The connection was there, and I knew I could talk with him for hours, but it was time for me to go home. I was about to leave and he leaned over to kiss me, but he caught me on the cheek since I had turned my head. He told me that when he first laid eyes on me 21 years ago as a teenager, he wanted me and always thought I was beautiful. He told me he would like to be my second man and spoil me. I wanted him, but I was with Tristan, and I let him know that I would never leave Tristan for anyone. You should never say never.

I don't know what came over me, but I grabbed his face and started to kiss him, and we ended up sleeping together. Yes, this was my first time cheating on Tristan and my first time having sex with another man since I got with Tristan almost ten years earlier. I felt indifferent, but that it was supposed to happen. It felt right!

The next day, Quincy and I talked on the phone on and off about what we had done, and I could sense that both of us were happy and wanted this to go somewhere. I already had love for this man, and I never felt this way about another man, and I know I never will. Quincy called me and asked me to come see him two days after what happened between us. It was Tuesday, July 2, 2019. We sat on his enclosed back porch, discussing what happened between us, how he would look at my pictures on social media, and how he wanted to be with me.

It started to rain, and we ended up having sex on his back porch. That night, when I went home, Tristan was in his office. It was rare for him to be there that time of night. I went in to tell him I was home, but I sensed something wasn't right.

The next morning, Tristan decided to go to the office building to work that day. He would always kiss me on my forehead before leaving for the office, but that morning, he walked out of the bedroom without saying a word to me. I asked him if everything was okay, and he said you know what's wrong. He did not have to say anything else. I knew he found out somehow that I cheated!

I decided I wasn't going to lie. Since our son's birthday party was that weekend, we discussed it Saturday evening. I was ready to talk, but Tristan wanted to watch the UFC fight first. I felt relieved because I had more time to think about what to say.

We finally sat down around 1:30 a.m. to have this conversation at our dining room table. Tristan looked at me, and I could see the anger in his eyes. He said to me, "So you decided to fuck and suck on other niggas!" I was shocked by those words because I never heard him speak that way, and he had never spoken to me like that before. I could not say anything except I did not suck on anyone, but Tristan said, "You fucked him." To lessen the blow, I told him that Quincy only gave me oral sex.

I found out that night he had known since Tuesday. He had activated the GPS on the Benz, got the address, and found out who owned the house. He went on social media and typed that name in, and it came up as a mutual friend, so he knew I knew Quincy. At first, he thought this was some random guy I met on Facebook. I let him know that Quincy was someone that I've known since I was 17 years old. I told him that in recent years, I only would socialize with him on social media by liking pictures and commenting on posts, until May 18, 2019, when we had a coffee date and started texting each other here and there. Tristan told me to leave. Although my hair was still wet from having just been dyed, I left in my pajamas and drove off.

I called Quincy around 2:00 a.m., and he answered right away. He asked what was wrong. I told him everything that had happened, and he told me to come to his house. I told him that wasn't a smart idea since Tristan would know where I was, so I drove around talking to Quincy until 3:30 a.m. Quincy asked me again if I wanted to come to his house, and I said no. He told me to drive back home because he did not want me outside in the middle of the morning.

I returned home, and Tristan was in our son's room in his bed. I stayed up almost all night. It was the calm before the storm.

The Big Blow Up

The next morning, Tristan said that he wanted to talk again, but he flew into a rage. I had never seen him like this before. He grabbed our family pictures, went out to the deck, broke the frames on a couple, ripped the pictures, and threw them down in the woods. I grabbed the main family pictures and ran into the house to hide them so he would not rip them up. He was screaming and cursing at me.

He called my parents and sister. This wasn't the first time he had done something like this—involving my family in our business to embarrass me and make me look bad. My dad is the type of person who doesn't want to hear it, and will not get involved unless someone is going to do something to one of his girls physically. My mom and sister came to my house, which worsened the matter. I did not want that added stress, so I drove off in my car. I had to drive into my yard to get out of my driveway since my mom had parked at the top of it.

I left the house with only a T-shirt, no bra, booty shorts, no shoes, and no phone. I drove to my friend Amy's house, but she wasn't home. Her neighbor came to my car to tell me she had just left. Once she saw me with tears streaming down my face and how I was dressed, she thought it was some domestic violence that I was just involved in, but I reassured her that it wasn't that. She went into her house and returned with some clothes that still had the tags attached. She told me to put them on and gave me a pair of slippers. She asked if I wanted to wait for Amy in her house. I thanked her and politely declined.

I wanted to drive around the corner to Quincy's house; he lived around the corner from Amy. I really needed him, but I did not want to go to his house unannounced, or let him see me in that state. I knew it would've made him angry. After driving around for about two hours, I returned home. My mom and sister were gone, and Tristan had calmed down by that time. It hurt my heart more than anything that my son had to witness the incident that had happened between us two that day. Tristan's behavior that day was entirely out of the norm, because we never had a "fight." Of course we had disagreements, but we would sit down like two mature adults and talk about our issues. This wasn't a normal situation. I cleaned myself up and went to the deck to talk with Amy. Her neighbor told her about me stopping past. I told her everything, but later, I discovered it was a big mistake.

Tristan cleaned himself up and left without my knowledge. I was glad he left because I wanted and needed time alone. I spoke to Quincy, and he was angry with me because he wanted me to come to his house, but it wasn't that easy.

My son was with my sister, but I told Quincy I needed time alone to think, and I would call him back later. Tristan did not come home until 4 am, and we did not speak for a few days. I was still communicating with Quincy even though Tristan made me delete him from my social media page and block him from my phone. Tristan did not know that Quincy had more than one social media page, but that would soon be revealed. I would still communicate with him through that page and delete the messages.

I went to Walmart and purchased a Tracfone. I gave Quincy the number, and I would use that to call and text him. I would charge the phone up at night by placing it in the garage outlet and removing it by morning. I would hide the phone in different places so Tristian would not come across it.

I know many of you are wondering why I was going through all this trouble to stay in contact with Quincy, and not trying to repair my 10 ½ years of relationship. It was because I knew it was already over, and I was deeply in love with Quincy.

Quincy's Baby Momma

After three months, I was still having this "affair" with Quincy and I could not let him go, and vice versa.

Quincy started having significant issues with his kid's mom. She was creating fake social media pages using Quincy's pictures, and starting a bunch of stuff trying to paint him in a bad light. She found out he was talking to me, and she contacted Tristan. She left a message to Tristan in his social media inbox, with my profile picture from my social media page, asking, "Is this your wife? If so, tell your cheating wife to leave my baby daddy alone. He doesn't want her, and he's only been using her since his last "girlfriend" left him in March." Tristan and Quincy's baby mama made a pact that if she found out any new information about me messing with Quincy, she would report it back to him.

Quincy and I thought it would be best to end what we had going on, so we stopped communicating with one another for about two weeks. I thought about Quincy during this time but I was trying to get my house back in order. We're not used to this kind of dysfunction. Things were quiet and peaceful. I can't remember if I contacted Quincy or if he contacted me, but we started talking on the phone again once in a while, but mainly through Messenger. Somehow his kid's mom found out and contacted Tristan through Messenger in November 2019. She told him I commented on a picture on Quincy's page saying, "Very handsome." This is how Tristan found out about the second page. She gave him the information, and he saw my comment when he went to the page.

He made me block that page, too. He was mad, but at the same time, he noticed that I commented on that picture a couple of months ago. By this time, without my knowledge, Tristan had installed spyware on our computer, and this wasn't the first time he had done this. Early on in our relationship, he spied on me through the computer, too. I wasn't doing anything to make him do that, but it showed that he was insecure for some reason. I'm bringing up spyware because that is how the next events unfolded.

I noticed Tristan was being very quiet and not speaking to me at the beginning of the week of December 11, 2019. That was normal. Some days he would not talk to me, or say very little. Sex was nonexistent.

December 20th was an exciting day for our son Henry. It was the last day of school before winter break, and I was coming to school to help with his class party. Yes, I was one of those hands-on moms who liked helping with school functions. It brought me so much joy, and Henry was always so happy to show me off to his classmates. The kids and I had so much fun, so I was pleased when leaving the school with Henry after the party. I told him I would order pizza or get KFC for dinner that night and watch a couple of Christmas movies as a family.

I knew Henry and Tristan had haircut appointments later that evening. I spoke to Quincy, who wanted me to meet him at the tattoo shop since he was getting the last details done on his tattoo. He also wanted to see me because he missed me, and I missed him, too. The plan was to meet him there after Tristan and Henry returned from the barbershop. I told Tristan to pick up dinner at KFC. Henry entered the house, and I went down to the basement to get in the car so I could leave. I asked Henry, "Where's your dad?" He said he had to go back to the barbershop to get his money. I knew that was a big lie.

I called Tristan to see what was up. Well, Tristan was going to an Airbnb to stay. He had already packed his Gucci overnight bag and had it in the trunk, so he planned to leave that day after getting their haircuts. He said, "You know what you did." This always confused me with Tristan. He would never tell me what I did. He would want me to guess, or try to catch me in a lie to find out if I did something else.

He did this a lot of times during our relationship. It's like he liked to play mind games with me. I found out where Tristan was from the Benz GPS app. I went up there and confronted him about what was going on. I thought he found out about the phone. I said, "Oh, is this about the phone?" He said, "What phone?" So I knew it wasn't about that, but the cat was out of the bag now that I had another phone. The real reason he left was that I was searching for a special Christmas gift for Quincy. The only reason he knew it was for Quincy was because he was a member of that fraternity. He asked me to leave, so I left and went back home.

I called Quincy, and he was mad at me, too, because I never showed up at the tattoo shop. I tried to explain what happened, but he said he wasn't trying to hear it because he really wanted to see me, so he hung up on me. I had Tristan and Quincy both mad at me for different reasons. All I could do was cry. I wasn't feeling right, got dizzy, and passed out. Henry called his nana, my mom, to let her know his mommy had fallen.

Henry called his dad, too, but he did not answer, thinking it was me calling. Henry knew that if anything ever happened, he was to call his grandparents and push the button on the alarm system for medical help, and that's what he did. I woke up in the hospital ER. After having a lot of blood drawn and tested, it revealed I had a mild heart attack! Tristan came to the hospital after my mom called him, but once they said that I'd be okay, he left.

I didn't talk to Quincy for almost a week. I called him on December 27th, but he was at a function and told me he'd call me back because he was worried about me. Quincy and I spoke, and I told him what had happened. He was sad that had happened to me, and he missed me. Over the next couple of months, Quincy and I did not have any physical contact, but we did talk on the phone and text here and there.

Tristan and I tried to do couples counseling, and that's when I found out the real reason Tristan said that he would never marry me. He held on to an incident between his mom and me after I gave birth to Henry. So, all these years, I finally knew why we hadn't married. What I could not understand was why Tristan proposed to me if he felt that way about the incident, because the incident took place almost a year and a half before he proposed to me. He admits that he should have never proposed to me.

At this time, the love I had for Tristan was damn near gone. I loved him only because he was Henry's dad. I knew my love for him was gone that night in November 2017 when he told me he would never marry me.

I did a Target run and purchased another phone because Tristan threw the other Tracfone I had in the woods behind our house. When I got home, I saw he had bagged up many of my clothes. He called my parents again and told them he wanted me out of his house. I went to my parents' house; I did not call Quincy. I did not want to involve him in this nonsense and needed this time to myself.

Tristan and I decided that our relationship was over. I could stay at the house until I found my own house. I always had good credit, so I applied for a home loan and was approved to purchase a home in the six-figure ballpark.

Quincy and I were back to seeing each other. Tristan went out of town, so I met Quincy at a neighborhood bar after a comedy show I went to with some female associates on February 29, 2020. We hadn't seen each other since the end of November, so I was nervous to see him. I got out of my car and proceeded to walk to his car. I wondered why he hadn't gotten out yet. When he finally did, he grabbed me and hugged me, and I returned the gesture. He said someone must've missed me, and I said, "Yes, I missed you a lot." It took him a little longer to get out of the car because he was video-recording me walking to his car. He wanted it on tape. We had a lovely evening, had a couple of drinks, and I left my car in the parking lot and got in his car.

We went to his house, talked, and we made love. I knew this was the man I wanted to be with. It had nothing to do with sex at all; you can get that anywhere. It was the fact we had a deep connection like I was made for him. It's hard to explain, but I just knew this was the man I should be with. We went and got some food, and he fed me. At the beginning of our "relationship," I loved this about him; he was romantic.

Two weeks later, Tristan was out of town again, so Quincy and I hooked up. He picked me up at my house. As soon as I got in the car, Quincy hugged and kissed me all over, telling me how much he missed me. He stopped a couple of times to kiss me again. We got drinks and wings. The bar was packed that night, and all of us were in there, not knowing the next day we would not be allowed outside for a long time.

I was so drunk that I could barely walk!

I returned to Quincy's house and we did not reach the bedroom. Right there in the recliner chair, he gave me oral sex and he made love to me in the hallway; it was very intense. We were both saying that we loved one another. It was not our first time saying that. It was our thing, and to this day, we still talk and say I love you even while having sex. I believe it got Quincy off to hear me say that I loved him.

The next day, I had lunch with my friend Amy. Quincy called to let me know that he found my earring on the floor, and I asked if he wanted something to eat. He said yes, so I got him some food and took it to him. I knew something was wrong. I'd come to see this look, and I did not like it because it always meant he was angry, or about to distance himself from me. He gave me a half hug and my earring. I gave him the food and told him I'd call him when I got home. He said thanks for the food and shook his head. He said okay.

Yup, there it went: "Rose, that was very intense last night; you're still with Tristan. I think we should just be friends." I started to cry because I loved this man to my core, and he continued to do this to me, but at the same time, I did understand because I was still with Tristan.

Later, I learned that one of the other reasons he cut it off with me was that he was still involved with his kid's mother, and had gotten back with another ex from his past.

Pandemic: 2020

We were full-blown into the pandemic now. Everyone was locked in their homes because of COVID-19. It had turned the world upside down. Quincy and I met up to take pictures of him for his website.

Quincy took a selfie of us. I did not know he had put this picture of us on his Facebook story, but his baby mama saw it and sent it to Tristan. Tristan and I got into it, so I left out and drove to Quincy's house because I wanted to know where I could find his baby mama, because it was time she got her ass whooped. I got up to Quincy's house and knocked on the door, not realizing it wasn't his second car in the driveway. He had someone at his house.

I got back into my car, and he came to the car, telling me to roll down the window. I was sitting there feeling like a damn fool. I jeopardized everything for this man while he was hanging out with another woman. All I could do was cry, and as I was pulling off, I looked at Quincy in the rear-view mirror, and with a sad look on his face, he yelled out for me to drive safely. I finally knew it was best for us to be friends or for me to distance myself from him altogether.

God or the Universe had other plans for what I needed as far as being in Quincy's life. I met Quincy in April, the day before Easter. I parked my car and hopped into his. We sat there talking. I could see that he wasn't happy. Deep in my heart, I knew he was depressed about things I did not know at that time.

I asked if he wanted to talk about it, and he said no, not really. My heart ached for him, and even to this day I don't like to see him hurt or in any pain. I could feel this man's energy and sometimes knew what he was thinking. We sat silently for about five minutes, which felt like an hour. I broke the silence by asking if he wanted some of the ham I had just picked up from the store, and he said no. He started talking a lot about what was happening to him and the crazy stuff one of his baby's moms was doing. It was the one that made that pact with Tristan in 2019.

I could not believe what I was hearing and to think someone would be that hateful. All I could do was say sorry that he was going through that and hug him tightly, hoping my hug would make things a little better for him, and let him know that I cared and loved him. I did not want to leave him like that, but I had to return home to Tristan and Henry.

The Harris-Johnson household had a nice Easter, but I still had Quincy on my mind. In the meantime, Digital Download, LLC was BOOMING!!! I was being pulled so thin then, but I did not complain. How could I? I was grateful that our family could still pay our bills, buy food, get takeout, and our 18+ employees and their families could still do the same. Tristan was working long hours, and I was working long hours, too! I had another job added to my long to-do list: production crew for Tristan. He started a virtual show with his high-powered clients called "The Show Down." I had to prepare him for this show since all barber shops were closed; I was the in-house barber, too!

Thank goodness I had a background in cosmetology, graduating from a reputable school in 2002. I would cut his hair, trim his beard, and set up the "stage." You would think with me doing all of this I would not want to do anything else, but I decided to put my nursing degree to use after 21 years.

I knew that many older adults would need extra care at that time, so I started working as a health aide/personal assistant. All my clients lived in the area, so I did not have to travel too far. I only worked on the weekends, so overall, I worked 7 days a week during the pandemic. I would help with personal care and household chores and run errands to the pharmacy to pick up their medicine and groceries. It was rewarding, and it was something I was doing for me. I knew I would need that extra money, too, since I was looking for a house and wanted to purchase my own vehicle without Tristan's involvement.

I would still make time to meet with Quincy to have coffee and coach him. I know you all are wondering how I had any extra time since I was homeschooling my son, working for Tristan's company, working my healthcare gig, and having meet-ups with Quincy. Believe me, it was a job, but I made it work.

When you feel so strongly about something, you can do it. I tried to make everyone happy, mainly my little Henry. I always knew there was a reason behind why Quincy and I became friends at that time in our lives, and I was about to find out why.

Quincy's Coach

Now that I was working my nursing job, I could steal some hours with Quincy by telling Tristan that I was working early or late. I met Quincy one Saturday morning in May 2020 before work to have tea with him at his house. I would park my car at my client's house, and Quincy would pick me up. I know what you all are thinking. "Wow, she was doing the most!" You all might have failed to realize that I finally felt alive again, and hadn't felt that way in a long time. No, I'm going to stop lying to myself. I never felt like this ever.

Quincy was my drug of choice, and I was addicted. If this was how a crackhead felt when they got that "hit," I understood why they would continue to do it knowing that it's bad for them to do. I'm not saying Quincy was bad for me, but it was bad because I was still living with Tristan.

Like I was saying, I would still meet up with Quincy. He felt it was best to meet at the coffee house instead of his home. I knew he was avoiding having sex with me since he was still involved with his baby's mom and another woman. I was okay with that because I felt there was more to our "relationship" than sex anyways. Not having sex never changed the way we felt about one another.

One day, I was on the phone with Quincy, and I'd been wanting to say a few things about his drinking a year prior but did not know how to go about telling someone that they had a problem. I understood how Quincy could be as well. This was the day I had to do it, because I knew he wasn't at his best right then. I asked him if he ever thought about doing a detox. I didn't mean a food detox but a detox of his mind, body, and soul. He was confused, and I laid it out on the table by telling him that he needed to do this detox from alcohol, fast food, and the multiple women he was sleeping with. I wanted him to give up the cigars and coffee, too, but he said, "Rose, come on, I got to keep the cigars and coffee." I let him keep his cigars and coffee. He later gave up the cigars in April 2022. I was surprised because he agreed to do it without protesting or anything. I think he knew it was time, and mainly since he wanted to do many good things in the community, he knew this was the only way to make a positive impact. You can't preach to people about things you're not doing in your own life.

Now, I just added coaching to my list of jobs, too. Lord, I was doing a lot during the pandemic! It slowed the world down, but it sped my world up, maybe because I wasn't living out my purpose, and this was a way for me to do that. One of the things I like to do is help people, and I finally had the chance to do so, and be of service to the people—one of whom was the man I was deeply in love with.

I would send Quincy motivational text messages every morning. I wanted to speak life into this man, ignite that flame within his spirit, build his confidence and self-esteem back up, and always let him know that he could do anything and be anything that he wanted to be. I started to notice that he was taking this seriously and started to do a lot of things to help with the journey he was on.

He finished the three-week challenge! I called him to let him know how proud of him I was. I remember crying because I wanted the best for this man, and I was happier when he told me he would continue this journey. I would still send him motivational messages in the morning, but it was time for me to go MIA for a minute to see if he'd be okay on his own. I did not tell him I was going MIA; I went silent. Plus, I needed some time for Rose. I was becoming drained since I was not practicing self-care. How could I serve everyone when my cup was running dry?

I knew I wanted to be with Quincy. I had never been so sure about something! I wanted this for myself. I got serious about looking for a house. I was looking at two to three homes a day. I knew Quincy would know I was serious about being with him if I purchased a house. At the same time, things were about to take a lot of crazy twists and turns, which I had never seen coming from Tristan, Quincy, and Amy. Yes, my so-called good friend Amy, who I had told everything to. **Warning: Watch who you tell your business to.**

I didn't see this coming. In June 2020, Tristan came to me and said that he was going to stay at an AirBnB until he could decide whether he still wanted to be in Pittsburgh. I knew he had already made up his mind, so I said, "Okay." He left and went to an Airbnb.

Father's Day had just passed, and I had purchased a few gifts for Quincy, so I called him to let him know that Tristan had left. I told him if he wasn't busy, he could come down to pick up his gift. He said he would stop over. He came past, and I did not know how to act around him at first since it had been some time since we last saw one another. He hugged me, and I kissed him, but he did not want to kiss me. He gave me a little peck. We talked for a good hour, and I gave him the gift bag that contained his Father's Day gifts.

He looked sad, and I knew I was sad. I got out of the car and looked back as he watched me walk up my walkway to make sure I had made it into the house okay. I looked out the window with tears streaming down my face as he pulled off.

Amy: The Fallout

Amy and I have known each other for over 30 years; our mothers are good friends and while we had always been "friends," we became *good* friends in 2017.

We would have lunch dates almost weekly, sometimes with another friend. We would always take turns each morning texting each other a quote or just a simple good morning. I never trusted females, so it was best to be solo at that time in my life. Having a good friend with whom I could finally have lunch dates and go decor shopping was nice. The pandemic had also stopped our lunch dates, but by August, it seemed like people were trying to get back to normal. I used to have ladies' nights, but once I saw that those women wouldn't even check on me to see how I was doing, I stopped having them at my house. I never have people at my home now.

I invited Amy over on August 13, 2020. It was a beautiful day for lunch on my deck. I cooked salmon/shrimp salads and garlic bread, had a fruit tray, and prepared a fruit-enhanced water pitcher. I loved to cook and host lunch/dinner parties since I was an event planner. We were sitting out on the deck, eating and talking. Since I'd been on my journey, I no longer wanted to gossip or hear about other people's affairs; if it was not beneficial, I did not want to hear about it. Amy loves to gossip, but I would change the subject so we could continue to talk about what was going on with our lives or current events. Amy would always go back to gossiping about people from high school that I hadn't seen since. That day, I knew I would be limiting my time around her. With where I was in my life, I did not want negativity and low-vibrating people around me. Also, I did not like how she would talk about another friend's mental illness.

A week later, we went to the park to work out. We ran into my friend Kel. Kel and I had been friends since 1995. We met in high school and remained cool for all those years. Kel was the only guy Tristan didn't mind me going to dinner or hanging out with. Tristan had hung out with Kel before, too. Amy knew Kel from high school, and they went out on a date several years back. He was trying to holla at Amy that day, and they decided to have dinner that Friday. Amy wanted me to come, too, but I was not trying to be a third wheel. After my spa day, I decided to meet them at an eatery on Walnut Street in Shadyside.

I should have gone home like I started to do, but this had to play out the way it was supposed to. They were there for about 30 minutes and already had their food and drinks. I ordered my food and a drink. It was strange because Kel started talking about this woman he'd been dating on/off for years, asking us if he should finally propose to her. Meanwhile, I thought he wanted to get with Amy. Amy started telling us about her cousin, who was cheating on her husband, but then she decided to start talking about what was going on with Tristan and me.

Kel knew some of what was going on, but not everything. Amy just kept going on and on about me cheating on Tristan with Quincy. It was uncalled for. I said to her, "Don't do that!" and she said, "Fuck you and Tristan. I don't care about y'all fucked up relationship!" I was shocked and hurt; if it had been anyone else, they would've had to pick themselves up off the floor. I wanted to punch her right in the face. Instead, I asked the waitress to box up my food and bring me my check. Kel gave me a look. What in the hell was that about? Kel said, "No, Rose, you're not going to leave until y'all fix this; y'all been friends for way too long." We did patch things up that night, but I knew things would never be the same. The Universe was not done yet; be careful what you ask the Universe for.

On August 19, 2020, I asked the Universe to remove anyone who no longer needed to be in my life. When I got home, Tristan told me he was going to an Airbnb in Atlanta because he would start looking for a house there. He thought I was out with Quincy because it was Quincy's birthday that day. I did make a pit stop at Quincy's house to put his gift on his porch, but I did not see him.

On August 21, 2020, my friendship with Amy and my relationship with Tristian were officially over. The crazy thing was that a friend warned me about Amy a couple of times, and my sister did, too. I did not listen to them. I think she was jealous of me all that time, because she wasn't living the life I was living. Before the cheating, she knew I had a good man in Tristan—a big diamond ring on my finger, a nice home, a child, a brand-new Benz, and a business. She, on the other hand, had a failed marriage.

Ladies and gentlemen, be careful who you tell your business to, and weed out all those snakes hiding in the tall grass around you. The Universe showed out by removing Amy and Tristan on that very same day within two hours.

Picking Up the Pieces

The Move to the A

At that time, I needed Quincy!

I called him, even though I knew he was dealing with some things involving his kids' mother. When we talked, he said it was best if we stopped talking. He told me he hated that it had to be this way because he really wanted to be with me. I cried and simply said, "OK."

Tristan moved to Atlanta while I was in Pittsburgh homeschooling Henry, working my nursing job, and still working for his business. At night, when my son was in bed, I'd sit in my room, cry, and ask the Universe for the answers I needed. I prayed to God for peace and happiness. It felt like he heard my cries—because each day, I felt a little happier and more at peace. I started smiling again, and the tears were no longer falling. At the time, I knew I had to get my life back in order. I had to pick up the pieces and move in the right direction.

I went and purchased a brand-new SUV without Tristan. He was going to buy me a vehicle, but I wanted to do it on my own. I did not need him. I had great credit, and without him knowing, I had saved money for my down payment. I walked in there and walked out with the keys in my hand. I was happy!

Tristan was buying a mansion: a 5,000-square-foot home with a pool, hot tub, workout room, and all the amenities. He wanted Henry and I to move down there, but I wasn't willing to reside in the same area as Tristan. He made it clear in the house that I would have my own living corridor. As we weren't in a relationship any longer, this was how we would ensure Henry still had both of his parents under the same roof. I told him I would move down with Henry. I felt I had nothing to stay in Pittsburgh for. Quincy was gone, and my parents and sister would be okay whether I stayed or not. The Universe had other plans for me!

I purchased Quincy a couple of gifts, and I took the one gift bag up and left it on his porch. His other item was delivered on October 30, 2020, so I drove up there to put it on his porch after leaving my sister's house. She lives about three minutes from Quincy. It was weird, but something told me to leave Quincy's house and go a different way. Who did I see when I got to the bottom of the hill? Quincy. He was letting me pull out, but I was looking at him. People started to blow on me, and I noticed Quincy mouth the word "asshole." I turned back around like "Oh, Quincy wants to call me an asshole!" I exited my truck, but he was still sitting in his driveway. He was surprised to see me and asked where I came from. I said, "You just called me an asshole." He hadn't realized it was me in my new SUV.

He was so happy to see me, and I was glad to see him. He gave me a big bear hug, lifting me off the ground a little. He was happy that I purchased the SUV I wanted because I kept telling him a year prior that I wanted the SUV. I wanted to let him know that I purchased it independently, so I showed him the papers with only my name on them. He told me that he had been trying to call me, and thanked me for his birthday gifts from two months ago. I forgot I still had him blocked on my phone, so I unblocked him and we went back to talking, but only as friends on

October 30, 2020. Once we started talking again, it was clear Quincy still had feelings for me. And the truth was, I still had feelings for him too. I couldn't move to Atlanta, so I decided to stay—because I wanted to be with Quincy. I also knew he felt some type of way when I told him I was leaving. I wanted to see if we could be something now that I was officially single. Tristan moved down to Atlanta without Henry and me.

I still don't understand why he got that big house, but he did. Henry and I went down to Atlanta for Christmas 2020. I helped Tristan get the house in order. Before I went down there, I used his money to buy everything we needed so I could decorate—with help from a friend I'd met on social media who lived in Atlanta. She designed the master bedroom. We had a nice Christmas in Atlanta, and stayed until after the New Year.

New Start 2021: Quincy and Rose

When I got back home, Quincy and I would talk every night. We would talk about Quincy's organization, and how a woman he met on social media who read his book helped him get the ball rolling. I was so proud that he got it up and running because that was one of his dreams. He was making an impact with a book he had written some years ago. At that time, it had been 11 months since we had sex. Tristan had gotten out of his lease, so he asked me to sell or give away all the office equipment and furniture at his office.

I asked Quincy if he wanted anything, and he said sure. I told him to meet me at the office on January 16, 2021. I hadn't seen Quincy in three months, so it was strange to see him, and I did not know how to act with him. I wasn't sure if I should hug him since we decided to be friends. We both came with Christmas gifts for one another. As he was helping me take apart some tables and chairs, I was staring at Quincy. I wanted him right then and there, but I did not want to mess up our friendship. After he finished getting his things, I walked him down to the main entrance, and he turned around, hugged me, and smacked me on my butt. As he drove away, I walked back into the building with tears rolling down my face. My love for him was still very much alive—I was still in love with him. Even without spending time with him, without sex, and us not talking for almost three months—the love did not die. We started to learn more about one another, and we started talking about the home projects we both had going on. We would spend hours on the phone bouncing ideas off each other or discussing the stages of our projects. He would call me at least five times a day. I loved it, and I believed he did, too. Of course, that would not last forever because it made us want one another more. Quincy started saying to me, "You know I can take care of you," and I would always let him know that he could.

I went to Quincy's house in April 2021. This was my first time there since May 2020. When he opened the door, I went in, and we embraced for a long time. It felt so good and so right to have his arms wrapped around me. I did not realize how much I had missed him since we talked daily, but I missed being right there with him. He showed me his updates to the house, and we sat out back talking for about an hour. When I left that day I knew I was ready to be with Quincy, and I was hoping he wanted to be with me, too. He even started calling me babe again. I was still calling him Quincy, while he would call me Rose, babe, or Mama Bear.

Tristan and I had stopped having sex a while ago, and I needed to be held. Quincy and I started talking about us having sex, or if it was even a good idea. I knew I wanted the whole man, not just the sex. Quincy did tell me that he slipped up in March 2021 and had sex with someone. I felt hurt even though we were just friends at this time. I still loved this man, so to think of him being with someone else made me feel sad. We decided that we were going to have sex on May 2, 2021. Quincy told me he would call me after he did some work for his organization. At 2:15

a.m., he texted me: "Are you awake?" I know he probably did this because he did not want to start having a sexual relationship again—and he had a few good reasons. I think I knew Quincy couldn't just have sex and walk away—because he had deep feelings for me, and he didn't want to get even more emotionally involved.

I ended up going up there. At first, I was going to continue watching Moesha and answer him later in the morning, but after 10 minutes, I responded to his text and told him I was up and went to his house. I was nervous as if it was my first time being with him. I was sitting on his bed in the dark. He came over to me and bent down to kiss me, but I gave him a little peck. He asked, "Should we do this?" I told him I didn't know. He said "You did not kiss me like you usually would." He bent down again to kiss me, and he said "That's how you typically kiss me." He started to undress me, and once he entered me, all those emotions came rushing back like a tidal wave. I could not hold it in any longer. I started to sob. He stopped making love to me, looked down at me, and said, "Rose, you're breaking my heart right now." He said we could stop and he would hold me, but I told him to continue. I loved this man so much and could not understand why I felt like I did about him.

Why had I never had these emotions or feelings for another man? All I knew was that I wanted us to be together, but that did not happen. We started having sex—not regularly, but more often than we had in previous years. After messing with Quincy for a long time, I learned his pattern. He'd be completely in love with me—telling me he loved me and that he wanted us to be together—but after about three months, he'd start to shut down. It was like he would get mad at me. Was he really mad with himself because he could not be with me the way he knew we both wanted to be together? I knew he had bad relationship traumas.

He would stop answering my calls, and he'd be slower to text me back. When he got like this, I'd start to wonder why—if I had done something to make him pull away. That's when my anxiety would kick into overdrive, and I'd start overthinking everything. I hated that feeling, and I wish he knew how it made me feel when he shut down like that. He could not be consistent at all, and I know he tried. On July 28th, 2021, I was at his house lying in bed watching a movie, when I said, "I could do this with you forever." He looked over at me and smiled. He looked at me and asked if I loved him. I then looked at him and told him "Of course I love you." He said "I love you, too" and kissed me on my cheek. I was happy, thinking everything was good. After the movie ended, he looked at me and told me we needed to talk. He said "I think we should take a break." I'm thinking to myself where the hell did that come from? He said, "Let's take a two-week break without talking, texting, or seeing one another." I told him, "You must want to lose me." He said, "Rose, how would I lose you in two weeks?" I told myself, "You can lose someone in one day." I agreed to this two-week break, so from July 28th until August 14th, there wasn't any communication.

My son was still visiting with Tristan for summer break and was due back home in two days. Of course it was quiet, and I had no friends except Quincy. I had associates, but not anyone I would call, talk to, or invite to my house. I would sit on my deck reading to pass the time since it was the weekend. I was happy to pick up Henry at the airport because my little boy would be home, and I'd have him to go places with and talk to. Henry and I love each other so much, too! I would have so much fun with my little boy—my Henry.

August 14th came, and Quincy texted me first thing in the morning, saying he had my wristband. I thought, is he serious? No "Good morning," no "Okay, our break is over now"—just a text about a damn wristband. Why did he not say "Good morning, I've missed you." I knew that he texted at 8 a.m. because he missed me. I went over that day to see him. I gave him an early birthday gift. I got a diamond-encrusted necklace customized for him. It had the three main things he's about on this chain. I put a lot of thought into that gift, and I'm glad he loved it.

I had a special day planned for his 43rd birthday. I made reservations at an upscale Brazilian restaurant in downtown Pittsburgh and purchased some very nice gifts for him. I always want my man to know that I respect him. I want to make him feel appreciated, happy, desired, and loved.

We got dressed up, had a lovely dinner, and returned to his house to relax while watching a movie. A week later, he asked for another week's break. I always gave Quincy the benefit of the doubt because I knew he loved me, but I knew it was hard for him to be consistent in a relationship with me. I knew he was not intentionally trying to hurt me, but he still ended up hurting me.

Black Hole: Sick and Tired

I knew Quincy was about to shut me out completely. I felt it, and I saw the signs. It became a pattern, and I learned to recognize and know it all too well. I tried to prepare myself, but how could you prepare yourself for the man you love to ghost you?

The phone calls completely stopped, and he only texted me occasionally. At the time, my son was being bullied at school, so that added to my stress level. Anxiety and depression were about to come up like they never had before. I needed Quincy at that time, but I knew he had a lot going on, and he made it very clear that he only had two things he had to think about: his boys and his book. I had to fight this on my own.

Quincy did try to be there for me when Henry got bullied at school by calling up to the school and speaking with the principal. He checked on me to see how Henry and I were doing, but that also stopped. It got so bad with the bullying that my son came home crying on October 16, 2021, and I packed our suitcases and hit the road. I drove 11 hours by myself with Henry down to Tristan's house in Atlanta. I hadn't been sleeping well—I'd only gotten about four hours of sleep over the past two days. I was glad to almost be at Tristian's house because I was falling asleep at the wheel. Since Henry was sleeping, I had to crack the window and turn the radio up louder, but not too much.

I would have never left if I had known Quincy would text me that night. I asked Quincy to call me. I did not want to lie to him even though I knew he was going to be angry with me, but I let him know that I was in Tennessee heading to Atlanta. I knew he was furious, but he tried to mask it once I told him why I was driving to Atlanta. Henry needed his dad and he wanted his dog. Quincy knew that Tristan did not know we were coming, and he kind of got mad. Unlike him, Tristan wouldn't get angry with me—his son's mother and ex-fiancée—for showing up unannounced. I know he would have talked me out of making that drive if he had known we were coming.

As I was on the phone with Quincy, I saw police lights and thought, "Shit, I was speeding," and I was about to get my first ticket! I let Quincy know, and he told me to get off the phone and keep my hands on the steering wheel. Being a Black woman, I was scared to be pulled over by the police, especially down here close to the Virginia/Tennessee border. The police were cool, and he did not get me for reckless driving since I told the truth when he asked me how fast I was going. I think I was going about 90; he said I clocked you at 88, so I got hit with a ticket for $335!

I texted Quincy to let him know that I got a ticket and was back on the road. He told me to text him once I got to the house to make sure Henry and I made it there safely. We got to Tristan's house at 6 a.m. I was praying that Tristan did not have a woman over because he was dating several women at that time. I punched the code in, and the door opened. Henry made a lot of noise once he saw his dog, so I ran upstairs to Tristan's room to let him know it was us. To my surprise, he was still snoring and alone. I woke him up, and he thought he was dreaming at first, but he quickly realized that it was reality. He said, "How did you all get here?" I let him know I drove and what was going on. He was happy to see Henry and glad we made it there okay.

I got Henry in his PJs, tucked him in his bed, and got into bed because I needed some sleep. I texted Quincy to let him know that I was at the house. Quincy told me to call or text him once I got up. When I got up, I texted Quincy, who told me to take care of my business. I told him I'd be back on Monday.

The Stay in Atlanta

Henry and I both needed this time away from Pittsburgh. Henry was happy to be with his dad and to play with his puppy. When I'm anxious or going through stress, I clean! I ended up cleaning Tristan's house from top to bottom.

Tristan took me to a restaurant/lounge because he knew I needed an outlet. It was a nice time for us to talk without Henry being around. I let him know what had been going on in Pittsburgh. He reassured me that everything would be okay, and that he'd be there for Henry and me. He knew that if I wasn't good mentally, our son would not be good either, and vice versa. We have a good co-parenting relationship. We do what's best for our son.

I was able to rest the next couple of days and recharge my battery. Of course, Henry did not want to leave, and we talked about him moving down and finishing elementary school there. We decided it would be best for him to finish school in Pittsburgh and start a fresh new chapter in Atlanta for middle school. I packed our suitcases into my SUV to head back to Pittsburgh. I texted Quincy to let him know I was on my way back. He texted back and told me to be safe and to keep him updated on our drive home. One thing I can say about Quincy is that even though I know he wasn't thrilled about me going to Atlanta, he still wanted to make sure we were okay, and that's another reason why I love this man; he acknowledged my son as well.

Henry and I got back home around 1:30 a.m. I let Henry stay home from school until that Thursday to rest up from that long drive. The rest of his school year was okay. He lost a couple of friends since kids his age were finding their way and dealing with peer pressure, but I'm glad my Henry stayed true to himself and started to stick up for himself.

Quincy and I needed to have a conversation once I got back. I went to his house, and it was not a good conversation. Quincy was angry that I went to Atlanta after I said I would not go back down there, but what was I supposed to do? My son wanted his dad, and Quincy wasn't available since he had a lot on his plate. Tristan was the one that I could count on at that time, and he was Henry's dad. Quincy sat there folding laundry, and I just stared at this handsome man I loved so much, but I could see the stress on his face. I know it wasn't just about me going to Atlanta. I'm overprotective of Quincy, and I'm not sure why because I'm not like that with all the people in my small inner circle, but more so with Quincy. I'm speaking about the adults. Of course, I'm very overprotective when it comes to Henry and Quincy's kids—my bonus kids, Jackson and Brandon.

I did not like the look on his face or his tone. I know he was frustrated with me, so he said bye, got up, and went to his bedroom. Normally, I would go after him, but I wanted him to have his alone time, so I left. I tried calling him later, but he did not answer. I left him a long text message telling him how I felt about him, and that I was sorry.

Turning Point

I was sitting at home bored, so I decided to go get a drink at Mad Mex in Shadyside. While I was there, I was thinking about Quincy. I texted him a picture of my drink and asked him what he was doing. He said he was in the basement listening to music, drinking coffee, and thinking. He asked if I still had some Henny, and I said yes. He told me to come over and bring it with me. When I got to Quincy's house, he had left the front door open, so I went down to the basement. He was sitting there, and he looked stressed, so I went over to him, hugged him, and kissed him. The last time I was there, I left two small bottles of Long Island Iced Tea, so he poured him some Henny, and we were both sipping on the Long Island Iced Tea.

We got into a heated conversation about me going to Atlanta, but I had to bring that to an end because I don't like to argue. It was irrelevant since Tristan and I were no longer together. I went down there solely for my son. Quincy looked at me and said in a firm tone I never heard him use before, "Don't play with me, Rose. And I'm drinking, too." I did not know what to think about his statement and wondered if that was a threat. He knew I had been in a violent domestic relationship before, so it made me uncomfortable and scared to think why he would use that tone of voice and the statement he made. I think Quincy could sense that and told me to come closer, so I went and sat on his lap. I reassured him that I loved him and would never leave him.

The next day, I went to a wedding, and I hadn't heard from Quincy, so when I left the wedding, I called him, but he did not answer. He ended up texting me to let me know that he was hanging with his kids and would call me later. Later came and went. I knew he'd been making excuses for weeks to see me instead of telling me the real reason for his sudden behavior change. I knew his old secretary had returned to the picture, and I always suspected she had a thing for him. He might have had some feelings for her as well since she was the one to help him get his organization off the ground.

I believe he got tired of me asking about hanging out. On November 28, 2021, he told me that he missed me but felt that we were both more focused on our businesses and that it was best for us not to hang out. I asked if we could still text, since he was the only friend I had—the only one I truly confided in—but he never responded.

That shattered my heart.

Suicide Attempt

If you recall, earlier, I mentioned that on October 31, 2021, I tried to commit suicide in my garage, but Henry saved me!

Henry FaceTimed me, and I promised myself I would not do that again. I had my notes written and everything. I was exhausted and disappointed about a lot of things. I had slowly sunk deeper into depression, but I still got up every day to get Henry to school, made sure I helped him with his homework, kept my house clean, cooked dinner, and kept my appearance up. As I previously stated, I was never depressed in the traditional way. I would never let Henry see me cry, so I would wait until I tucked him in bed, and I'd be in my room on the floor crying to the point I could not see.

I had been going through therapy at that time for 2 ½ years, but I did not tell my therapist about all that was going on until one day, I knew it was time to do the hard work to start healing. I let my therapist know what was happening, and we devised a weekly plan. We started breaking down everything, beginning with a little before I was born.

We laid the foundation for me to build my way through the healing process. I'm not going to lie; healing is hard as hell, but it's worth it. I'm not all the way where I want to be, but I'm stronger. I know my worth, know that I'm enough, and know that the storm does not last forever.

I would like to thank Quincy for pulling away from me because if he had not done it, I would not be on this journey to heal from my demons. It was a blessing in disguise. As I write this on October 6, 2022, I'm still in therapy and healing, and I'm becoming a stronger and a better woman for it.

Fighting for Love

Back in December 2021, I decided to fight for this love with Quincy. I felt he was worth it and knew he was who I wanted. Even Tristan thought it made perfect sense for me to be with Quincy. Tristan, and a good friend who I helped years prior, were there for me when Quincy and I weren't speaking. I really needed that kind of support. Tristan is an amazing man because he did not have to be there for me at that low time, but he knew our son, Henry, would not be good if I wasn't okay.

I wrote Quincy a four-page letter and sent him a card that I never got the chance to give him. I mailed the letter and card to him. I explained to him how I felt about him and how I wanted to be with him. I apologized for causing him any pain or confusion. Of course, I did not hear back from him, but I wasn't expecting to hear back from him. That's another thing I learned in therapy: never expect anything. You will be less disappointed if it doesn't happen.

Christmas was just around the corner, and on Christmas Eve, I got a weird feeling that something was wrong with Quincy. The night before, I could not sleep and kept thinking about him. I could feel his energy coming through to me strongly. I decided to look at his Facebook page, and from his post that morning, I learned that he had COVID-19. All I could do was cry, and I dropped to my knees right there in my living room and began to pray for him. It pained me to see how he looked and could barely speak, but he was still being the good man he was by speaking on a serious topic.

I had purchased Christmas gifts for him and the kids long before Christmas, and I was going to take them up to his house and leave them on the porch, as I had done with previous gifts when we weren't speaking. I had to do something because of who I am and my love for Quincy. I went to the store and purchased him some orange juice, ginger ale, and some cans of soup since I wasn't sure if anyone had gone to the store for him, or if he had gotten store delivery. I called, but he did not answer. He texted me right back to let me know he had COVID-19 and was in bed. I told him to come to the door to get the bags I had left on the porch. He texted me to thank me for the items and that he was returning to bed.

Quincy texted me on Christmas afternoon to say Merry Christmas and thank me for the gifts. I ended up spending Christmas alone since Henry was in Atlanta with his dad, and I did not really feel in the Christmas spirit. To make myself feel a little better, I put up the Christmas Tree and decorated it while listening to traditional R&B Christmas songs, while sipping on a glass of wine.

I was happy to speak to my little boy to tell him Merry Christmas, and I could not wait until he got back to open his presents. Tristan and Henry got me a lovely Christmas gift card, which brightened my day. My parents called to wish me a Merry Christmas and to let me know to come pick up my gifts. They asked if I wanted to have dinner at their house, but I declined since I wanted to be alone. I went a couple of days later to exchange gifts with my parents.

Once Tristan and Quincy were gone, I started to get all these DMs from men from my past. I'm a private person, so no one knew about my situation at all, and I barely used social media. A guy I was communicating with, whom I'd known since elementary school, called me asking if I finally wanted to hang out with him. I told him I'd call him back. At that time, there were two men, including the one from elementary school, with whom I was communicating, but I knew I was only doing it to fill a void that Quincy had left. I deleted their numbers and blocked them when I hung up with the guy from elementary school.

I was not going to go backward! I was pretty messed up in my 20s, even though I did not look messed up. I was hopping from man to man when I would not receive what I needed or wanted from one. What I wanted was simple—just a nice man to be friends with and get to know.

However, I would continue to meet men who only wanted to sleep with me because I was pretty. Some I slept with, and some I did not sleep with. I knew I was only sleeping with those men to feel wanted and not lonely.

At 41, I did not want to revisit that vicious cycle. Of course, when I was with Tristan, I didn't mess with anyone else until I got with Quincy. We were together for 10 years when I "cheated," and by this time, I'd been messing with Quincy for almost three years, so no way did I feel comfortable being around any other men, and I couldn't imagine sleeping with anyone else. I've only been with two men for almost 14 years.

Since I was spending Christmas alone and declined my parents' invitation to dinner, I ordered dinner from an upscale Brazilian restaurant. I went to pick up my food and came back to have dinner with a few glasses of wine. I tried to be okay, but I kept thinking about Quincy, thinking about how this was the first Christmas we could've spent together. I ended up passing out that night in the living room from drinking a whole bottle of wine by myself.

New Year 2022

On New Year's Eve, I went grocery shopping because Henry was coming back home the next day. I was driving to Virginia to pick Henry up from Tristan on New Year's Day. Like I said, I could always feel Quincy's energy. I was on my way back home from the store. Wines and Spirits did not have the wine I wanted, so I drove to another Wines and Spirits that was closer to Quincy's house. As I was coming up the hill to leave the shopping center after getting my wine, Quincy was driving down the hill, and he blew his horn. I did a U-turn and went to see where he parked. I found him, got out of my car, and walked over to his car. He opened his car door, and I asked why he was out of bed. Well, they had new guidelines for COVID-19, and he had met those guidelines.

He got out of the car, and we had a long embrace (he was wearing a mask, and so was I). He ran into the store to grab what he needed, came back out, and we proceeded with our conversation. He asked what I was doing for New Year's Eve, and I told him I would be alone since Henry was with Tristan. I asked him if he wanted to bring in the New Year together. He said that could be possible since he would be staying in, but he still needed to disinfect the house.

He told me to call him at 8 p.m. I called him at 8 p.m., and he texted me that he would be going to lie down. I was disappointed, but not too disappointed since I already knew it wouldn't happen. Remember I said I learned in therapy to never expect anything; it will leave you less disappointed.

I drank a glass of wine and went to bed at 9:30 p.m. since I had to get up early to make the trip to VA. I set my alarm to midnight to call to wish Henry and Tristan a Happy New Year, but they beat me to it. I talked to Henry for five minutes, and cried myself to sleep thinking about Quincy. The next day, I was happy to see my baby boy, and we got into my SUV to head back to Pittsburgh. I texted Quincy to wish him a Happy New Year but did not hear back that night. Then, a few days later, I saw him at our kids' school, as he was already in line. I had to ride past him to get to my usual spot. He blew the horn at me and texted to tell me good morning, and that it was him blowing at me. All I could do was shake my head. If you can't answer my text messages, don't blow the horn or text me when you see me in our community. Keep that same energy!

I was going extra hard with therapy, and every day I got stronger. I could feel the healing taking place. I was about to do the craziest thing to get Quincy back. I was a woman fighting for love. I was scared, and did not care how I looked doing it. I was living with no fear or self-doubt. That was my mantra for 2022. That morning, before taking Henry to school, I knew Quincy was going to be at the school dropping the kids off. I put this card I got for him in my coat pocket, and I knew I was going to give it to him by all means necessary. As you all can see, I have a true, genuine love for this man. Plus, I got a psychic reading in January, and she told me that he and I were soulmates and that I should fight for him.

When I got Henry into school, I saw Quincy pulling from the curb, so I stepped out in the middle of the road. He had no choice but to stop. He rolled down his window. I grabbed his face, told him I loved him, gave him the card and a hug, kissed him, and walked away. The strange thing is that it felt as if everyone going in and out of the car rider's line and taking their kids to the door were at a standstill. Not one car pulled up behind him, and that's unusual since there are about 200 kids who are car riders. Maybe God slowed everything down for us. From that day forward, I knew I would fight for our love.

I got him something for Valentine's Day and asked if I could come over to give it to him, and he said yes. The date was February 19, 2022, and it was my first time in his house since October 24, 2021. The strange thing was that I did not feel different with him. We were in his room on the bed talking. I took my clothes off and left my panties and bra on. I got under the covers, and it felt so good for him to pull me close to him. I needed his touch, his body against mine, his smell; it was something I craved. I think most people would not understand that intimacy outweighs sex. Of course, he's a man and tried to have sex with me, but I moved his hand because that wasn't what I wanted at that time. I wanted and needed his closeness. Without speaking, I knew he was cool with him just lying there and holding me. He pulled me closer, and I fell asleep in his arms. That was the first time I could sleep well in those five months. We ended up hanging out for about three weeks after that. It was a beautiful day in March, so we decided to meet up for a couple of drinks. It was his first time out since his birthday seven months prior, which was also the last time he had an alcoholic beverage. We got to catch up and talk about what we'd both been up to. He told me how he felt about me and said he wanted to heal so he could truly reciprocate the love I had for him. I thanked him for loving and respecting me enough to walk away rather than use me for sex. I told him it still hurt not to have him in my life. I was a mess that night going home, but I was also relieved that deep down within him, he still cared about me a lot. He used those words, but I knew that man loved me.

Tristan was fading out of my life since he was in a new relationship. We would only talk about our son. I did not feel any kind of way about him moving on; I was happy he found someone with whom he had a connection since he did not find that with me. Most women would be jealous or mad, but I'm a secure woman, and I know that everyone is not meant to be together. It's life! I wasn't his person, and he found someone who was.

When Quincy and I met up in March, I had told him about signing up and paying the deposit for skydiving. I had wanted to skydive since forever, and I used to try to get Tristan to agree to do it with me, but he wasn't with it. I was happy in May when Quincy agreed to do it with me, so I paid for his deposit and signed him up in the same time slot as me. The crazy thing was there was only one available spot left. I believed it was fate for him to have this experience with me. It was a beautiful day on June 19, 2022, three days before my 42nd birthday, and it was Father's Day when we skydived! I can truly say it was a life-changing experience to jump out of a moving airplane at 13,500 feet. You will never be afraid of anything, not even death, because you just stared death right in the eyes. As a birthday gift, he paid for my jump and pictures, too! I would say this was the best birthday gift I ever received. Although Tristan has given me many nice birthday gifts over the years, this was something that I always wanted to do, and it's kind of like a once-in-a-lifetime experience. Quincy and I were thrilled that we skydived! We got a chance to share that experience together, which was a form of intimacy.

Still Fighting

As of July 16, 2022, Henry had moved with his dad to attend school in Atlanta. It was hard for him to adjust since Tristan moved his girlfriend and her son into his home. Henry was the only child and always had his dad to himself. Of course, it was different when I was with Tristan because I would not compete with Henry for Tristan's time. I'm going to get Henry therapy because I don't want him to be in his 40s seeking help from a therapist because of childhood traumas that could've been addressed in his childhood. We must break those cycles and get our kids the help they need while they're still kids. I want the best for my son; and he knows he can return home if he no longer wants to be there.

My relationship with Tristan will never be the same, as too much has happened. I still want the best for him, and I see him as family since we have a child together, and will one day have grandkids as well. We had a few disagreements, but the new me tried to make it work because it was about our son, not our feelings. I was still working at Digital Download as his senior administrative assistant and was very active within the company. To the best of our ability, we co-parented to make it work for us all, including our new relationships.

As for my relationship with Quincy—as I sit here writing this on November 4, 2022—he said he thought we needed space. I found out on Halloween 2022 that, for years, he had been dropping hints about not wanting company or it not being a good time for visitors. I'm actually glad this happened, because now I understand why he always had that moody vibe. I guess he was never planning to have an honest conversation with me about it.

What I still don't understand is why I had to figure it out through hints, instead of this 44-year-old man just telling me he wasn't up for company. I would never get upset or take it personally if someone told me they didn't want company. It would've made life so much easier—and we probably wouldn't even be in this situation.

    I replied to his email, and I didn't hear back. It had been four days. I was no longer chasing after him; he'd contact me when he was ready. I had a lot going on. On October 26th, 2022, I was diagnosed with Stage 1 anal cancer, and I would have surgery on November 9, 2022, to remove it. Again, Quincy went MIA when I needed him, but I knew Quincy's main priorities were his kids and his dreams. That's what consumed him and fueled his go-getter mentality. He rearranged his day to take me to get my one procedure done. I appreciated and loved him for being caring and thoughtful in doing that much for me, but I needed him to be there for me emotionally. He did better this time around. He made time for me, helped me with things, and bought me small gifts. I appreciated him for really trying to have a normal relationship with me. Before this happened, I had been falling back a little so I wouldn't get hurt too badly if he decided to go in another direction and no longer included me in his life.

    I know after Quincy, there will not be any other. I would rather be alone and happy than date multiple people trying to find the right man for me. I'm not having sex with any other men. In my opinion, that's one of the ways you must find out if someone is a good fit for you. I could not be with someone who could not please me sexually. Quincy did a great job keeping me happy in that department. Plus, I had only been with Tristan and Quincy within the last 13 years. I'd been sexual with Quincy for three and a half years, so yeah, there will not be another man touching me. I would never be happily single, but I know I can learn to be happy alone.

    I'm still in therapy, and I have an amazing therapist. She has helped me be able to navigate this life better and heal from my childhood traumas. Most of those demons I had were no longer active in my brain; they had to be evicted. I can say that therapy truly works; if you put in the work, it's worth it. I highly recommend it. Now, when I feel down, I take a walk, or listen to my music and dance. If I were spending time with Quincy, we'd talk about it. I find peace with him and feel at home with him, both of which are feelings I did not have with the other men I was in relationships with. He calms my soul. I can be myself around him. Besides having a connection, we do have things in common, and we have differences as well.

I think it's good to have a combination of likes and dislikes. It can be boring to be with someone if you both like everything the same. It teaches you how to compromise; and there's got to be balance. Quincy and I were in the process of learning each other's love languages, and it felt great learning together as a team. Our intimacy was getting better by the week. I have faith that we will come back together and be stronger. We must learn to communicate effectively and not be afraid to say what's on our minds.

If you are reading this, babe, I want you to know that I respect you, desire you, understand you, see you, and, most importantly, love you!

Conclusion

I love me in my 40s—this is when you start living! I know there's been some ups and downs so far, but one thing I'm happy about is that I was able to get rid of a lot of those demons that held me back for most of my life. I will continue picking up the pieces to complete the puzzle of me.

I will also continue working hard on my dreams and goals as I approach the next decade of my life.

I'm not fully healed, and I doubt if I ever will be; but I have the "tools" and knowledge to deal with stressful and disappointing situations when they arise in my life.

I wrote this book as part of my healing process, but I also wrote it to help girls and women who have gone through—or are currently going through—a storm know they have a voice.

If you are being molested, raped, or are currently in an abusive relationship, know this: you have a voice, and you are strong enough to get help. There are many resources available to support you.

Stand tall, fight for yourself, and don't be afraid to ask for help!

Acknowledgements

I want to thank the following people who made this journey possible:

- **To my wonderful Sonshine** — thank you for being my greatest joy and biggest accomplishment. Your curiosity, creativity, and boundless energy remind me to embrace life with an open heart. Watching you grow and discover who you are fills me with pride and hope for the future. Always remember that you can achieve anything you set your mind to. There's no ceiling in how high you can go. Love you, you're my world!

- **To my dad** — I would like to take a moment to express my deepest gratitude to you. Your support, love, and belief in me have been the foundation of my journey. Thank you for teaching me how to stay strong through any circumstances, for the value of resilience, for always encouraging me to follow my dreams, and for being my greatest inspiration. I am forever grateful to have you by my side. I'm always going to be a daddy's girl. Love you!

- **To my mom** — thank you for being my guiding light and one of my biggest supporters. Your love, encouragement, and belief in me have shaped who I am today. You have taught me the importance of kindness, strength, and perseverance. I am forever grateful for your presence in my life. Love you!

- **To my sister** — thank you for being a constant source of positivity and encouragement in my life. Your support, infectious laughter, and boundless love have uplifted me during challenging and joyful times. I am grateful for the bond we share and the countless memories we've created together. You inspire me to be my best self, and I thank you for being on this life journey with me. Love you!

- **To my son's father** — TFJ, thank you for the decade we shared together. Through the highs and lows, I have learned so much from you. Our journey has shaped the woman I am today, and I am grateful for the experiences and lessons we've shared. While our paths may have taken different directions, I appreciate the role you continue to play in our lives and the bond we will always share with our son.

- **To EBJ, my love** — the man who inspired me profoundly during these last five and half years, thank you for your love, support, and inspiration. The memories we created and the lessons we learned together will always hold a special place in my heart. We have seen each other through many seasons and been through a lot together. Your influence has shaped my journey in ways I will forever cherish. As I always said, as I was helping you, you were also helping me. I am grateful for meeting you all those years ago. I'll love you always & forever.

- **To my bonus sons** — I love you two so much. You two have brightened my life in so many ways over the years. I want you both to know that I'll always be here for you and always love you. Remember, there's no ceiling on how high you can go.

- **To my therapist** — thank you so much for helping me work through my healing process and giving me the tools to navigate this world more positively and effectively. Also, thank you for reminding me that my traumas do not define me and that I'm worthy and enough.

- **To Publishing Peer Consulting** — thank you so much for helping me throughout this experience of becoming a self-published author. I'm very appreciative of the countless hours you spent helping me make my book great and achieve one of my goals! You worked on my book like it was your very own. Also, thank you for your professionalism. You're the best!

- **To Nicole Myers, RN** — I wanted to take a moment to extend my heartfelt gratitude for being a beta reader for my memoir. Your support and insights were invaluable to me during this process. I appreciate the time and effort you took to provide thoughtful feedback, and I truly value your encouragement and belief in my story. Once, again thank you!

A Letter to the Reader

Dear Reader,

I want to take a moment to acknowledge the courage it takes to confront difficult experiences, whether they are your own or those reflected in my memoir. If my story has brought up feelings that are overwhelming or painful, I want you to know that you are not alone, and I've provided a few resources on the next page.

It's completely understandable to feel triggered by the topics of domestic violence and sexual assault. These are heavy subjects that can evoke strong emotions, and I want to emphasize that your feelings are valid!

Thank you for being part of this journey with me. Together, we can continue to support one another and empower ourselves and each other.

With love and strength,

Rosemary Harris

National Resources

The resources listed here are for informational purposes only. I am not affiliated with these organizations, and inclusion does not imply endorsement.

National Domestic Violence Hotline
https://www.thehotline.org
866-799-SAFE(7233)
Text "Start" to 88788

RAINN
National Sexual Assault Hotline
800-656-HOPE (4673)
Text HOPE to 64673
https://rainn.org

Suicide and Crisis Lifeline
Call or Text "988"
https://988lifelife.org

About the author

Rosemary Harris is a passionate mental health counselor, mentor, and entrepreneur behind A Helping Hand Coaching, LLC. With multiple degrees from Point Park University and The Life Coaching Institute, she is dedicated to providing support and guidance to individuals seeking to enhance their personal and relational growth. Rosemary believes in the transformative power of connection and is committed to helping others navigate life's challenges with compassion and resilience.

In her spare time, Rosemary enjoys traveling to different countries and has a deep love for '90s R&B music, often attending concerts that take her back to her favorite era. She resides in Pittsburgh, PA, with her teenage son, who inspires her every day.